LOVE ON HOLD
WAITING ON THE MAN OF GOD

CINTIA STIRLING

ISBN 979-8-9856938-3-6 (Digital)
ISBN 979-8-9856938-4-3 (Paperback)
ISBN 979-8-9856938-5-0 (Hardcover)

Love on Hold
PO BOX 692207
San Antonio, TX 78269
www.loveonhold.com

Any italicization or words in brackets added to scripture quotations are the
author's additions for emphasis and clarity.

Printed in the United States of America First Printing, 2022

—— ♡ ——

"God's love is unconditional, sacrificial and everlasting;
and He is the only reliable way to find a spouse
that loves us this way."
- Cintia Stirling -

—— ♡ ——

Acknowledgements

This book could not have been completed without the help of some very important and special people, and I would like to thank them.

First and foremost to God and His Holy Spirit, You inspired this book from beginning to end. You put your words in my heart; I just wrote them on paper. Thank you for entrusting me with this project.

To my dear husband Caleb, you believed in the calling God put on my life. Without your support, this book would not have been possible. Thank you for making me feel like the most loved and cherished girl on earth.

To my editor Suzanne Zucca, you did to my manuscript what is done to an uncut diamond: you removed all the rough spots until it was polished. I admire and appreciate your work. Thank you for blessing this book with your wisdom.

To my parents, Patricia and Cesar, it is because of your love, sound advice, and correction that I received the blessing of a godly spouse. Thank you for your prayers.

To my dear furry friend Chloe, who was always by my side as I spent endless hours writing, her tender love is truly a gift from above.

Last but not least, to all the women who shared with me the stories that have been included in this book, thank you for opening your heart. May God use your testimonies to bring hope, guidance, and encouragement to many single people.

CONTENTS

INTRODUCTION

I remember the night this book was conceived in my heart. I was in my bedroom, crying out to God, "Why, God! Why! I can't believe you have created love to be this hard." I was angry, devastated, and heartbroken. Despite all my efforts, I was not getting this one thing right: finding a godly man with whom I could fall in love and who loved me unconditionally. I was looking for someone who was willing to go down on one knee and commit to me, marry me, and live together happily ever after. Isn't that the dream of every Christian single woman? Well, it was mine too. But it wasn't happening.

My clock was ticking as I approached that terrifying age I had set for myself with fearful thoughts like, "If I don't get married before this date, I have already lost my chance to find love and start a family." I had grown tired of the mess of dating and getting my hopes up just to be disappointed over and over again. "What am I doing wrong?" I thought. "God, what do I need to do that I haven't done yet? Please show me! I have no idea why this is not working for me. I am going to give this matter completely to You and wait for You to show me the way," I said. "I promise You one thing: the day that You bless me with my husband, I am going to write a book for every single woman to know the way You allow love to happen. "

Little did I know that all of those years as a single in waiting were God's preparation, not only for Him to introduce me to the love of my life, but also for this book to come to fruition. It wasn't until I courageously moved in faith and obedience to God that I met my husband. And not just any husband, but the man that God had destined for me.

We all want to do things God's way. No one sets out to initiate a dead-end relationship or to marry the wrong person. We all want to find that everlasting, unconditional love that seems to be scarce or nonexistent in today's society. We all have made mistakes. However, if the desire of your heart is to find God's path to love by seeking His will and submitting to Him, He will provide that person in His timing. Through Him, everything is possible.

Finding the right path of love with God is a journey that is a privilege for every single believer to go through. For some time, God may put your *Love on Hold* to equip and prepare you and your significant other. Once His time has come, and as you walk in faith as He leads you, you will be ready to receive, enjoy, and take care of the love He has blessed you with.

You might think, "Oh no! I don't want to wait anymore. I have been waiting for a long time!" Behold, my dear friend, this *Love on Hold* journey is everything but passive waiting. It is a preparation that will require effort, commitment, perseverance, courage, self-denial, faith, action, and yes, patience as well. If you want God's best, there is no other way around it. You could still possibly find love by doing your own thing, but how is that working out for you so far? Even if your way works, what do you think the chances are of lifetime success, or that it will be a love that will grow stronger over time? Only God can do that.

You don't want your love life to die in front of your eyes. You don't want to rush your decisions just because you feel your clock is ticking, neither do you want to settle for someone that God never intended you to be with. No, you want the Creator to lead you, to open doors for you, and to close the ones that you should never step through. You want Him to amazingly prepare that divine encounter with the man that you have dreamed of all your life— your husband.

If you are single, I want you to find the kind of love that is real and lasts, love that withstands the test of time. This is the kind of love that God planned for all of us. It does exist, it can be found, and most importantly, you deserve it. Maybe you have already gone through the heartache of several broken relationships. Maybe you are frustrated, desperate, and wounded, and have gotten to the point of thinking that real love is very hard to find or may not exist at all. Maybe you have even questioned what is wrong with you, or what is wrong with the people you have dated. You might have come to conclusions such as, "I am not good enough," or "I need to try harder." But the truth of the matter is that God never intended love to be this hard.

The love challenges that I faced and that the great majority of singles are facing are the result of a broken model from the broken world we live in. *Modern dating* was never part of God's plan. Why? For the same reasons that you and I already know—modern dating is complicated, messy, confusing, lacks commitment, and often leads to emotional pain and sin. A better model of finding love is the one that God designed from the beginning, where there is purity, commitment, honor, and intervention of the Holy Spirit.

I wrote this book with every single woman in mind. If you are single and actively dating, single but haven't dated in a long time, single but have never dated, divorced, widowed, or living with your boyfriend but not married, this book is for each and every one of you. This book is also as much for the single teen starting to explore the avenues of love as it is for older singles in their thirties, forties, and beyond. I know that your journeys and experiences in love are all very different depending on your age, status, and culture. However, two things are universal, never change, are never wrong, and apply to every single case no matter what—God's Word and the guidance of the Holy Spirit. This book is full of them both!

God has given me an important commission, to speak His truth into your life and to help you in your journey to find love. I am confident that this book will be a resource that you will find yourself referring to often and will be indispensable in your walk as a single woman. I know that as you go through the pages of this book, you will find yourself reflected in it. May you be blessed and encouraged by the biblical truths and stories that you will find here. I hope that by the time you have finished reading, you will decide not to blindly pursue love anymore, but to courageously follow God's lead. Dare to believe that He will orchestrate and graciously unfold your love story as you step forward in faith.

With much love,
Cintia Stirling

CHAPTER 1

FIRST LOVE

The decision was already made. I only needed to wait three months to graduate from university; pack my bags; and leave behind my family, friends, and country to start the journey to a new life with the man that I loved. I was in love, or at least that was what I thought. The relationship seemed promising; it was exciting, fun, and passionate. We were very young. I was twenty-one and he was twenty-three. Even though distance separated us, nothing seemed impossible, or complicated; we were determined to fight for our relationship.

The plan of moving to another country, however, had its own set of challenges. First, I hadn't bought a plane ticket because I didn't have money, because I didn't have a job. Second, I didn't have a permit to live or work in the country where I was planning to move. I had met this "true love" in Canada while I was studying abroad. So naturally, the plan in my young mind was to live and work illegally, at least temporarily until I figured out how to become legal. Third, I had neither the support nor the permission of my parents to leave. For them, my great idea was something completely stupid and overly dangerous. However, none of these things were a concern for me because nothing was going to stop me from leaving.

My plan was the following: once I arrived in Canada, I would live with my boyfriend so I wouldn't have to spend any money renting an apartment. I would look for a job, one that could pay me under the table, maybe in a restaurant as a waitress or in a nightclub as a bartender. I would figure out how to become legal later. Everything was resolved! That was what I thought. I was anxiously awaiting the day of my graduation with excitement and expectation. I was dreaming about the day that I would be next to the man that made me happy. However, in those three months leading to my graduation, something happened that completely changed my plans and the course of my life forever: I met God.

My encounter with the transforming and unconditional love of Christ happened in 2006. He revealed Himself in my life right before I would lose it irreparably. I didn't know the danger of doing what I was about to do, neither had I pondered the potential consequences of my plans, but God knew everything. He knew the end from the beginning, and He knew that the path that I was about to take was not going to be anything good for me.

One spring afternoon, just a couple of months before packing up and leaving my home and family forever, I heard God's voice for the first time. He said:

> Cintia, my daughter, in this time, I have been bringing rescue into your life. The enemy has come and has tried to seduce you. He wants to divert you from my purposes, presenting you a path that seems to be good but ends in destruction.
>
> You have been trying to walk in that direction, and you have felt frustration because you haven't been able to move forward. There are obstacles that prevent you from going ahead. What stands in your way is my hand that is trying to stop you from continuing in that direction.
>
> My daughter, I have plans, good plans, for you. If you surrender your dreams to me, I will open a path for you where there is none. I will fulfill the deepest desires and longings of your heart. In the meantime, I want you to be submissive to my hand, and I want you to abide in my

will. Abide in me and I will give you the future
that you are hoping for.

If you listen to my voice today and you
abide in me, one day, you will be ready to go, and
you will know when the time has come because I
will reveal it to you. And I will go with you, and
I will bless you because you put your trust in me.

While God was speaking these words to me, I felt a burning
sensation in my heart. I thought that I had known love with the guy
I met in Canada, but that love didn't compare, not even slightly, to
the love that God was letting me feel in the midst of His presence in
that moment. God's voice was loving, full of mercy, and compassion.
All my life I had walked far from Him without seeking Him. I didn't
even think about Him, but He didn't seem upset or offended by that.
In His voice, I could feel His embrace, His love, and forgiveness, like
a loving father who receives his daughter with open arms.

What God was asking me to do in that moment was extremely
difficult—letting go of all of those plans and dreams, letting go of
that love, seemed wrong. It didn't make any sense to me. My heart
was conflicted. I felt that I loved that man, and it caused me pain just
thinking about giving up that relationship. But God was warning me
that there was danger in the decision that I was planning to make.

The Bible says:

> There is a way which *seems* right to a man
> and *appears* straight before him, but its end is the
> way of death. (Prov. 14:12, AMP)

Although my plans seemed good to me, if they were going
against God's will, they were not going to be good at all. They were
actually going to bring destruction to my life. In his book *Good or
God?*, John Bevere put it this way:

> It doesn't matter how good something
> looks, how happy it makes you, how much fun

it is, how rich and successful you'll become, how deeply spiritual it appears, how sensible it seems, how popular or accepted it is – and the list goes on and on. If something is contrary to the wisdom (or Word) of God, it will ultimately be detrimental and bring sorrow to your life.[1](24)

God was giving me a warning sign: "The enemy has come and has tried to *seduce* you." Satan was using with me the same seduction that he used with Eve in the Garden of Eden. God had said to Adam and Eve that they could eat from any tree of the garden, except from the tree of knowledge of good and evil. Satan came to Eve, seduced her, and tempted her to eat right from the forbidden tree.

> When the woman saw that the fruit of the tree was *good* for food and *pleasing* to the eye, and also *desirable* for gaining wisdom, she took some and ate it. She also gave some to her husband, who was with her, and he ate it. (Gen. 3:6, NIV).

Please look closely at this scripture. When Satan tempted Eve through seduction, the object of temptation had three traits. It was something that *looked good*, had a *pleasant appearance,* and was *desirable*. That was exactly how the man from Canada with whom I was in love looked. *Seduction is* what the enemy is using today with many young singles by presenting men and women to them who have the appearance of something good, attractive, and desirable but who, in reality, are being sent to deviate them from the plans and purposes of God.

In that moment during which I needed to make such an important decision of whether I should leave or stay, all of these things about seduction and temptation were not as obvious and evident to me as they are now. I didn't know how the enemy worked. I didn't

---

[1] Bevere, John. *Good or God?* Messenger International, Inc., 2015, p. 24.

know what to do. I didn't want to let go of that relationship; however, I didn't want to disobey God either.

"God, do I really need to do this? Do I really need to let go of all this?" I dared to ask God. Maybe he could arrange things for me, and make it all work for good.

"No, you don't have to do it," He said. "The decision is yours."

After that, I did not hear God's voice again for a while, although I sought Him several times to get more answers. Maybe He remained silent just to wait and see what I was going to do. Questions and thoughts invaded my mind for several days. On one hand, I was stubborn and wanted to continue with my plans; and on the other hand, the excitement and expectation that I was feeling at the beginning were fading. Something had become very clear to me—to pursue that worldly relationship and to leave my home and country were not part of God's plan.

After some time of struggle, I finally made the decision to surrender all of my plans, including that relationship to God. I didn't know what God was preparing for me later on, but He had promised me something: "If you surrender your dreams to me, I will open a path for you where there is none. I will fulfill the deepest desires and longings of your heart." The deepest longing of my heart in that moment was to meet a man that loved me deeply and unconditionally and that I could love the same way in return. I thought that this longing would be fulfilled in that relationship I was in, but God was showing me that was not going to be the case. He had something better in store.

I decided then to set my eyes on the promise that He was giving me and let go of that love that I had been pursuing. From that moment on, my focus was no longer to pursue the love of a man, but to know and deepen in my love for The One who loved me first.

Your first true love starts with God

I have started this book by sharing the first part of my story because I know that the message God gave me in 2006 is the same message that He has for each one of His single daughters today—a

17

message of *love, rescue, hope,* and *promise.* I know that there are many single women that probably identify themselves with that same deep longing for love that I had when I was single. They have been looking for love everywhere with despair and haven't been able to find it. Some have left everything behind to pursue it and have been deeply hurt and disappointed, others are in very stressful relationships in which they don't feel loved and cherished, and others are in even more difficult situations in which they do not know what to do.

In the years following giving up that relationship, I discovered that the only one who can truly satisfy the hunger and thirst of love that we all have is God. Before He gave me a husband, He first taught me to find my contentment and fulfillment in Him and to continuously surrender all my needs and desires to Him. After a few years, the time came in which God saw fit to give me His promise, a husband that came from His hand. By the time this happened, I had been transformed into a person who finds her emotional fulfillment in God and not in the arms of a man. The needy, desperate, and emotionally unstable woman that I was before knowing God was gone. The wounds from my past had all been healed by God. I was ready to move forward with boldness and without fear, embracing with faith and gratitude the blessing of the husband that God was giving me.

The need for love springs from the depths of our being because we have been created in the image and likeness of God and He is love. *Our first love relationship should not start with a man, but with God. He created us single so that we can know Him deeply by putting all our attention on Him, love Him completely with an undivided heart, and become one with Him before we become one with another person.* His plan from the beginning has been to live in an intimate and close relationship with us.

He perfectly knows and understands our longing for love, for having a partner that gives us affection and brings us protection. He knows our need for sex and intimacy; but He also knows that we will not be able to enjoy any of these things and appreciate them in the fullness of how He designed them unless we are first filled and transformed by His love.

Adam was the first single man in the history of creation. God had created male and female of every species, but Adam was a single man. The Bible says that there was not found a companion or helper suitable for him (Gen. 2:20). Had God forgotten Eve? The story can make us think that God did not realize that Adam would need a companion until later. But that was not the case. God does not forget anything; He knows the end from the beginning. Eve was always in the mind of God as the companion of Adam even before Adam was created. *God created man first and presented his wife to him later on purpose so that man would first learn to know, love, and obey his Creator.* Adam first needed to deepen his relationship with God in order to carry out the purpose for which he had been created before he was presented the blessing of Eve. Eve, on the other hand, was going to need a man who would be able to seek, hear, and obey God since she was going to be under the care, protection, and authority of Adam.

From the beginning of creation, God revealed a very important order: the relationship between God and man took place first; the relationship between man and woman took place second.

Maybe you've spent a long time looking everywhere for the love of a partner. However, it will not be until you start an intimate and personal relationship with God that you will know what true love is. Only then will you be able to love fully as God has loved you and enjoy the romantic love of a partner in the way God designed it to be: pure, passionate, free of fear, complete, and unconditional.

Marriage is the plan and design of God

If you have been single for a long time, maybe you have wondered if you are destined to get married one day. This question is on the mind of many singles. I asked it to myself several times through the course of my singleness, even when God had given me a promise that one day He would bless me with a husband. However, as the years went by and I didn't see that promise fulfilled, my faith at times started to grow weary and was attacked by doubt. The idea of remaining single for the rest of my life was not in my plans, but I didn't rule out the possibility.

However, every time I thought about remaining single, it caused me distress, sadness, and affliction. "Is it possible that God will not give me a husband even though I want to get married?" I asked myself, "Why would God put such a desire in me to get married if He wasn't going to fulfill it?" As I studied the Bible and learned that God says marriage is His plan and His design, I started to change my way of thinking and left my doubts aside. I began to declare the promises I found in His Word and believe that they would be fulfilled in my life. I started to pray according to what God had said, and not according to the doubts and fears that the enemy was sowing in my mind about a future full of loneliness and sadness.

> "Haven't you read," Jesus replied, "that at the beginning the Creator 'made them male and female,' and said, 'for this reason a man will leave his father and mother and be united to his wife, and the two will become one flesh?'" (Matt. 19:4–5, NIV)

Jesus reminded the Pharisees that God's design from the beginning of creation was that man and woman would be united in marriage. Marriage is a representation of the love of Christ (the groom) for His church (the bride). When a man and a woman are united in marriage, they glorify God. God created marriage so that when man and woman become one, they reflect in that union the love of Christ for His church (Eph. 5:25–27).

The Bible does describe four instances, however, in which some people will not get married. The first instance is due to a lack of *maturity*. When the Bible speaks about maturity, it refers to our spiritual growth as believers in Christ.

> But Jesus said, "Not everyone is *mature enough* to live a married life. It requires a certain

aptitude and grace. Marriage isn't for everyone."
(Matt. 19:11, MSG)

Being a mature believer and having the character needed to assume the responsibility of marriage is key to being able to receive that blessing. God is the source of true wisdom and maturity. As we draw closer to Him, gain knowledge of His Word, and learn how to apply spiritual truths in our lives, we will obtain the maturity needed to receive every promise and blessing that He wants to give us. My goal during the course of this book is to help you acquire wisdom from the Word of God concerning singleness and marriage. As you acquire wisdom, and the Lord reveals His Word to you, and as you take Him at His word, maturity will result.

The other three instances that the Bible describes in which a person will remain single are due to a *gift of continence* (or celibacy) and they are explained in the following scripture:

> Some, from birth seemingly, never give marriage a thought. Others never get asked— or accepted. And some decide not to get married for kingdom reasons. But if you're capable of growing into the largeness of marriage, do it.
> (Matt. 19:12, MSG)

In the first case, some people will not marry simply because they have never wanted to; they were born with a natural predisposition to be single. In the second case are the people who, for one reason or another, may not be invited to be married because of some existing condition that prevents it. And in the third case are the people who have decided to remain single voluntarily in order to fully dedicate their lives to serve God. The Bible mentions that if someone has the *gift of continence* and decides not to marry, he or she does right in remaining single because in this way, they can focus on the Lord's affairs and how to please Him (1 Cor. 7:32–24).

However, I think that if you have this book in your hands, it is because you want to find love; you want to get married. That means that you don't have the *gift of continence*. Therefore, unless you lack *spiritual maturity*, it is God's plan and design that you have a husband.

A hope and a promise of love

God didn't design love to be as complicated as we know it today. We have complicated love because we are not seeking God in the process. However, for all of those who are longing to find the love of a partner and receive the blessing of marriage, there is hope, and the Bible is full of promises of blessing.

The hope

> "For I know the plans I have for you," declares the Lord, "plans to prosper you and not to harm you, plans to give you *hope* and a *future*." (Jer. 29:11, NIV)

God has plans of good for us to give us a hope and a future. These two words have a great meaning on their own. *Hope* means that there is something better that God has in store for those that trust in Him; *future* means that the story has not yet come to an end. In this scripture, God assures us that for those who trust Him, He has the power to change their tomorrow and give them a future of good. It doesn't matter what their present circumstances are or what their past looks like. He is able to give them what their hearts have longed for. However, the plans that God has for us do not just happen on their own. It is necessary that we seek Him so that His thoughts and His ways will be revealed to us.

It is very shocking to see what is happening around the world among singles that are trying to find love. One study revealed that, "The average woman will kiss 15 men, enjoy two long-term relationships and have her heartbroken twice before she meets 'The One.' She will also suffer four disaster dates and be stood up once before she finally settles down with the man of her dreams. She will also have been in love twice; lived with one ex-partner and had four one night stands."[2] These statistics reveal that for most people, it is not only very hard to find the right partner, but it is also a messy process that normally involves lots of heartache and disappointment.

On the other hand, for those that have succeeded at getting married, numerous reports demonstrate that almost fifty percent of all marriages in the United States are ending in divorce or separation, and let's not even get into the details of how dysfunctional other marriages are that have not gotten to that point yet.

Being single has its own set of nasty statistics as well. "In America, almost half of new births are to unmarried mothers. The number of parents living together but not married tripled."[3] "Sixty-seven percent of Americans think that premarital sex is morally acceptable."[4] "More than seventy percent of women have had two or more sex partners before walking down the aisle. And statistics now say that only five percent of new brides are virgins."[5] Do you think that this was God's plan? No, it wasn't His plan at all! God says in His Word:

> My people are being destroyed because they
> don't know me. (Hosea 4:6, NLT)

---

[2] News agencies, "Average woman will kiss 15 men and be heartbroken twice before meeting 'The One', study reveals." *The Telegraph*, January 01, 2014, http://www.telegraph.co.uk/news/picturegalleries/howaboutthat/10545810/Average-woman-will-kiss-15-men-and-be-heartbroken-twice-before-meeting-The-One-study-reveals.html. Accessed November 17, 2016.

[3] Hanes, Stephanie. "Singles nation: Why so many Americans are unmarried." *The Christian Science Monitor*, June 14, 2015, http://www.csmonitor.com/USA/Society/2015/0614/Singles-nation-Why-so-many-Americans-are-unmarried. Accessed November 17, 2016.

[4] "Americans' moral stance towards sex between unmarried persons in 2016." *Statista*, https://www.statista.com/statistics/225947/americans-moral-stance-towards-intercourse-between-unmarried-partners. Accessed December 5, 2016

[5] Wolfinger, Nicolas H. "Counterintuitive Trends in the Link Between Premarital Sex and Marital Stability." *Family Studies*, June 6, 2016, http://family-studies.org/counterintuitive-trends-in-the-link-between-premarital-sex-and-marital-stability. Accessed December 5, 2016.

When there is no knowledge of God and His Word and our plans are imposed over His plans, the result is suffering, calamity, and destruction.

As I am writing this book, it is almost twelve years to the day that God spoke to me to warn me that the decision I was about to make was going to lead me straight to failure. What would have happened if I had not sought God during that time? Or what if I hadn't obeyed His voice? I am sure that I would have left my home, I would have moved to another country, I would have lived in free union with my boyfriend, we would have had premarital sex, I probably would have gotten pregnant, and we might have eventually separated, both of us hurting, both of us left in pieces, both of us becoming more statistics telling the story of the broken model. The story goes on and on. Everything would have been a complete disaster. But God stopped me because He had mercy on me. He showed me that He had a better plan, a future of good to give me even more than what I was expecting, and I embraced that hope.

He has a future of good for you too, my precious single woman. It doesn't matter what your past has been or what your present is, God can change your tomorrow and give you the future that you are hoping for. For God, it is never too late to bring rescue, healing, and restoration.

The promise

> Seek the Kingdom of God above all else, and live righteously, and *he will give you every-thing you need.* (Matt. 6:33, NLT)

The Bible is full of precious and exceedingly great promises. In the scriptures, we can find promises for descendants, financial provision, freedom, deliverance, healing, restoration, a better future, salvation. But nowhere in the Bible can we find a promise specifically linked to the provision of a husband or wife. However, what the Word of God does say is that He will give us *everything we need* as we seek first and above all things His Kingdom and His righteousness.

For many, having someone to love, and being loved, is a need and a desire of their soul and their heart. This need for love and companionship is also included within the things that God has promised He will give to us; they will come as a result of seeking Him first.

The promises of God, especially the ones that will greatly impact our lives, such as a spouse, a child, a career, a ministry, could take a long time to come to pass. It is possible that for us, they seem to be taking too long, but that's not the case for God. *In fact, if we wait patiently and confidently in God's timing, we will be able to accomplish and obtain many more things and blessings in a fraction of our life than what we could accomplish and obtain without God during the whole course of it.* Everything He does has a plan and purpose whether we understand it or not. He will first prepare us to receive His promises so that when He gives them to us, we will cherish them, will be good stewards of them, and won't spoil them.

You might be facing many of the challenges and emotional struggles that I, as a single woman, faced too. That's why I perfectly understand that your journey to find love has not been easy. But take heart, dear woman of God; do not lose hope. You are about to discover God's plan for love in the coming chapters. Everything that I learned from my personal experience in walking with God and from the many single women who have shared their stories with me has been captured here. It is my prayer that the Word of God will demolish wrong ideas and concepts that you had about love and will give you the direction you need to be ready to receive the blessing of a husband.

CHAPTER 2

SURRENDERING YOUR DESIRE FOR LOVE

There I was, holding on to nothing else but the hope and the promise God had given me. I had surrendered everything to Him: my life, my relationship, my plans, hopes, and desires. I felt it was the end of all I had dreamed of, but I was wrong. Surrendering was just the beginning of a transformational process God was doing in me—a process that almost every believer will have to go through in order to see God's will fulfilled in their lives.

Surrendering means submitting your will, your plans, your ways, dreams, and desires to God so that His will can happen. The expression "to surrender" is commonly used in Christianity; however, the Bible uses expressions such as "to offer," "to sacrifice," "to give up," "to submit," "to take up your cross," and "to deny yourself." All of these expressions describe what *surrender* means. When God asks you to surrender something to Him, what He basically is saying to you is this: "Leave this matter in my hands, let me take control and work things out for you."

I believe that every Christian single that wants to receive a spouse from God will have to go through the process of surrendering a love relationship or the desire of being in a relationship. It might not make any sense to you, and perhaps it is going to be emotionally difficult. But God knows what's best for you. When you surrender, you are trusting that His plans and His ways will bring forth a much better outcome than if you do things your way.

Disobedience is an obstacle

It is very important to obey God when He asks you to surrender a relationship to Him. Disobedience will become the first obstacle to receiving the promises that He has in store for you.

Let's take a look at Casey's story.

— ♡ —

Casey was a thirty-one years old lady who found herself in a long-term relationship. She wanted to marry the man she had been dating for several years and fervently prayed for that to happen. However, that man had a lukewarm attitude; sometimes he appeared to be very committed to the relationship, and sometimes he was completely indifferent. Sometimes he was very affectionate and attentive, at other times he was distant. This situation made Casey feel very insecure and confused.

As time went by, things did not improve. Casey began to pray and to seek God's guidance and the advice of her parents regarding this matter. In several ways, God showed her that this man was not His plan for her and that she should surrender that relationship to Him. After some time of emotional struggle, Casey decided to trust God, and she ended the relationship.

The next couple of months were extremely difficult for her; she was devastated and heartbroken. The man that she had spent years of her life with didn't fight for her heart at all, which only confirmed Casey's fears that he was only wasting her time.

A year later, Casey met someone that would eventually become her husband. This man pursued her, fought for her, gave her his full attention, respected her, and honored her parents when he asked them permission to be their daughter's boyfriend. Today, she is happily married to a man who adores her. She never imagined that she would be so happy and that God would bless her with such a special husband.

—— ♡ ——

From Casey's story, we can learn a few things. If she hadn't surrendered that relationship to God, she wouldn't have been available to meet the man that God had in store for her. Casey might have wasted years of her life in a relationship that was going nowhere. How many singles commit this great mistake! They waste precious years of their lives in relationships that are not worth the time and effort.

Through her obedience, Casey demonstrated to God that it was more important for her to please Him than to satisfy her deep desire to continue in that relationship. Her faith was fully in God and not in her circumstances. She did not let herself be dominated by the fear of loneliness or by her age concerns. Finally, we see that God rewarded Casey's faith and obedience by bringing a man into her life that far exceeded all her expectations. She realized that what she had let go of didn't compare at all to the blessing that God had for her.

Tested, shaped, and strengthened

When we completely surrender to God everything we are, everything we have, and everything we long for, blessings and rewards will come as a result. There are three things that happen in the time of surrender. Your faith will be tested, your character will be shaped, and your trust and dependence on God will be strengthened.

Your faith will be tested.

These trials will show that your *faith* is genuine. It is being *tested* as fire tests and purifies gold. (1 Pet. 1:7a, NLT)

Throughout the Bible, we can find many instances in which God *tested* the faith of men and women before He fulfilled His promises and brought forth His blessing. In Genesis 22 God tested the faith of His servant Abraham when He asked him to offer his beloved and only son Isaac and sacrifice him as a burnt offering to Him.

Surely, Abraham's heart sank in pain. Maybe Abraham scratched his head and wondered, "Hadn't God promised He would greatly multiply our offspring? How could this ever be possible if He wants me to offer Him my only son Isaac?" The Bible tells us that the next morning, he got up early and went to the place that God had shown him for the sacrifice. He did not delay, he didn't meditate for several days on whether to do it or not, he didn't enter into reasoning to run away from doing the task that he had been asked to do. No, he humbly *obeyed*.

God never had in mind to take away Abraham's son; in fact, God hates human sacrifice. What God really wanted to do was to test the faith of Abraham and make sure that he would not *withhold* anything from Him. This proved that Abraham loved God above all things, even above his love for Isaac.

In the end, God *provided* a ram for the sacrifice, and Abraham offered it instead of his son (Gen. 22:13). *When God asks you to surrender what you love most to Him, it is because He already has a provision ready for you.* God will provide. He will not keep anything that you have surrendered to Him without rewarding your faith, your obedience, and your faithfulness.

> Then the angel of the Lord called again to Abraham from heaven. "This is what the Lord says: Because you have *obeyed* me and have not *withheld* even your son, your only son . . . I will certainly bless you. And through your descendants all the nations of the earth will be blessed— all because you have *obeyed* me." (Gen. 22:15–18, NLT)

Abraham's greatest sacrifice to God was his *obedience*. God was pleased when He saw that Abraham loved Him and trusted Him enough to be willing to give up what he loved the most—the promised son he had waited so long for.

Now take a moment and think about this: Who is your Isaac? What is that thing or who is that person standing between you and God, and competing for the place in your heart that belongs to Him? Maybe it is a relationship or your desire to be in a relationship. Maybe it is something that you consider extremely important. Whatever it is, if God asks you to give it up to Him, are you ready to surrender it? Are you ready to let it go and let God do His will in your life?

Going back to my story with the man from Canada I was in love with, I could see that this relationship had become my Isaac. It was a relationship I cherished deeply, one that I thought I couldn't let go. I didn't want to give it up, yet it was competing for the place in my heart that should be focused on God. When I felt that I needed to surrender that relationship to God, I knew that He had the power to bring that man back or to replace that relationship with something better.

The reason I knew I had to surrender that relationship to God was because it was in sin, and we were unequally yoked (that man was not a believer, neither did he want to become one). Those things demonstrated that I was walking outside of the will of God. I could have decided to continue in it, but I knew that walking outside of God's will is a form of sin. Therefore, there would be consequences, and His blessing was not going to be in it.

I surrendered my Isaac (my relationship) to God, and He did not bring him back because He knew that man wasn't the best thing for me. God instead blessed me with an amazing husband years later, but that would not have been possible had I not been willing to surrender my desire for love to Him.

When you surrender something or someone to God, you must be ready to let it go completely and put it into God's hands, knowing that two things can happen: God will give you back what you surrendered but in a transformed, improved, enlarged, and restored manner; or He will give you something completely different, something far better and greater than what you had. In any case, He will *provide*; God's blessing will come as a result of your obedience.

Your character will be shaped.

> Because you know that the testing of your faith produces *perseverance*. Let perseverance finish its work so that you may be *mature* and *complete*, not lacking anything. (James 1:3–4, NIV)

When God tests our faith, He does so with a purpose—that we *persevere*. The word *perseverance* comes from the Greek work *hypomenō*, which means, "to patiently endure."[6] When we surrender something to God, it is hard to persevere during the waiting time with the right attitude: trusting in God with steadfast prayer; and maintaining a godly attitude despite discouragement, obstacles, and difficulties. This is exactly the type of character that He wants to shape in us before He trusts us with His big plans and His most precious blessings. Perseverance will produce in us *godly character.*

Often times we think that God is going to respond in our timing and in our way. When this does not happen, we lose heart. We become discouraged, and we even get angry with God if we don't see an immediate answer to our needs or desires. But the truth of the matter is that God never arrives late. God uses that time of waiting, if we surrender to Him, to develop maturity in us.

If we say that we have surrendered something to God and then we complain that we have not received an answer from Him, it is like not having surrendered anything at all. When we surrender, it is necessary to trust fully that God will do His work, that He will provide, and that He will make a way for us in His perfect time and manner.

We can delay seeing the fulfillment of God's promises if we don't keep the right attitude during the waiting season—an attitude of gratitude, obedience, and steadfast trust in God. To illustrate this,

---

[6] Richards, Lawrence O. *New International Encyclopedia of Bible Words* (Grand Rapids, MI: Zondervan, 1991), p. 484.

we can learn from the Israelites' journey through the desert. God had delivered the people of Israel from the yoke of slavery. Israel had suffered four hundred years under the oppression, mistreatment, cruelty, and abuse of the Egyptians. God came down, rescued Israel, and brought them up out of Egypt. He told them that He would bring them to a land of prosperity where they would no longer be slaves, the *Promised Land* (see Exod. 3: 7–8).

However, to get to that land, the Israelites had to cross a desert. It would be a difficult road, but it was not a very long one. As they walked toward the Promised Land, they began to complain. The walk through the desert did not come free of trials and struggles. Their hearts, throughout their entire journey, were stubborn and rebellious.

> They said to Moses, "Was it because there were no graves in Egypt that you brought us to the desert to die? What have you done to us by bringing us out of Egypt? Didn't we say to you in Egypt, 'Leave us alone; let us serve the Egyptians?' It would have been better for us to serve the Egyptians than to die in the desert!" (Exod. 14: 11–12, NIV)

This story parallels the journey of the single person in many ways. There are single people that behave just like the Israelites. They put their trust in God and believe that He will bless them in due time with a spouse. Then they start getting discouraged when they see that the promise is taking time to be fulfilled. After that, they lose faith, and they turn away from God. They stop waiting with the right attitude. Instead of obedience, they go off on their own: getting involved in new relationships without seeking God's guidance, having sex outside of marriage, and doing many other things their way. Then they wonder why God hasn't blessed them, why things are not working out. They start to complain and rebel against God just as the Israelites did:

> Why did you ask me to give up my relationship? Haven't you promised you would bless me? It would have been better for me to keep that (troubled) relationship I had, than being lonely as I am right now! (Paraphrased version of Exod. 14:11–12 applied to *Love on Hold*)

If we are inconsistent in our faith and we do not strive to have the right character and attitude of complete trust in God during the waiting time, we will delay our blessings; we will not be able to get to our own Promised Land.

My dear reader, has not God already shown you His glory and mercy? Do not let your stubbornness delay your blessing or make you lose forever what God has promised you. Even if you do things your way and succeed in finding someone to be in a relationship with, perhaps without knowing it, you are letting go of God's best. You might end up with someone who was never meant to be yours and who does not even compare to the blessing that God had planned for you.

The main purpose of waiting on God is to die to our own fleshly desires, to let go of what we want in the time, and in the way we want it, so that by denying ourselves, God will be exalted and glorified; and our dependence on Him will be made more complete. This time of waiting will bring purified hearts and characters, which are shaped to reflect more and more the character of Christ—a character of love, meekness, gentleness, humbleness, and complete submission to the will of God.

Your trust and dependence on God will be strengthened.

> The Lord your God, who is going before you, will fight for you, as he did for you in Egypt, before your very eyes, and in the wilderness. There you saw how the Lord your God carried you, as a father carries his son, all the way you went until you reached this place. (Deut. 1:30–31, NIV)

Indeed the wilderness (desert) is a place of dryness and need, a place of isolation and loneliness. Through the course of our lives, God will take us through spiritual deserts so that we grow stronger in our trust and dependence on Him. Through our journey in the wilderness, we can be confident that we are not alone. He will lead us and hold us along the way as a loving father that takes care of his child until He takes us to our Promised Land.

Singleness can feel like walking through a desert because of the feeling of loneliness, unmet expectations, and emotional pain. It might not be easy especially as we get older. Yet singleness is a blessing. It is a stage of life that God designed to prepare us and equip us for the purposes He has for our future.

Have you ever met someone greatly used by God who did not first have to go through a waiting period or have to surrender his or her plans to God? In the Bible, we see countless examples of people who had to go through times of isolation in their lives through trials and difficulties. Jesus himself was taken to the desert for forty days before he could complete his work of the redemption of humanity, and in the desert, he was tested. It seems that everyone who wants to be used by God in a great way will have to go through a time of waiting first, a time that seems to be of loneliness, but that is nothing more than a time of being set apart and prepared by God.

It took seven years from the moment that I gave up my life to God until the moment that God blessed me with my husband. During all those years, I was praying for him. Waiting was not easy; there were moments when I felt I had lost all hope. I felt sad, and many times, I was tormented by the fear of being single for the rest of my life. But then, with no other alternative, I continued to trust God and persevered in faith. I set my eyes on the promise that one day, if I continued to surrender my desire to Him and obey Him, He would be faithful to bless me with a spouse. At the end of those seven years, I was able to appreciate the wisdom I had acquired and the character that God had shaped in me as I spent those years seemingly in solitude, thinking that nothing was happening.

His preparation during my singleness is today so vital for the success of my marriage and for the fulfillment of my calling. Had

I not gone through all that time of waiting, this book would have never come into existence. Today, I understand that one of the purposes for which God took me through such a long waiting time was so that one day, I could share everything He taught me with you. I wouldn't be able to understand your pain or to sympathize with your need for love if I had not gone through my own journey. God uses the waiting time to prepare and equip us to fulfill His purpose in us.

We should always be confident that God loves us and that He will lead us to the path that is best for our lives. He will give you the kind of man that you need, and He will do so in His perfect timing when you are ready. *God will sometimes withhold our temporal satisfaction or pleasure in exchange for giving us the everlasting one. Sometimes it will seem like we are stuck in the same place, not making progress in our life; however, He is working in our behalf, for His will to be done and his purposes to be fulfilled.*

If you are currently single, be assured that God is doing something in you and in the person who will be your husband. He is preparing both of you; maybe there are things that God wants to accomplish first in your life while you are single. He is certainly giving you maturity and wisdom, and is teaching you to depend completely on Him.

When to surrender a relationship to God

You might be wondering how you will know if God is asking you to surrender a relationship to Him. There are three common ways to know when your relationship is not in the will of God and therefore will need to be surrendered:

When the relationship produces sorrow in you.

> The blessing of the Lord makes a person rich,
> and *he adds no sorrow with it.* (Prov. 10:22, NLT)

According to the above scripture, if the relationship you have is a blessing that comes from God, then there should not be *sorrow* or affliction with it because the will of God is *good, pleasant,* and *perfect* (Rom. 12:2).

Sorrow can come in many forms such as sadness; constant doubts; and feelings of confusion, anxiety, fear, insecurity, and lack of peace. You might also have significant communication problems with your partner, or continuous fights and arguments. All of the above are examples through which God might be telling you that you are not in the right place or with the right person, and that you need to walk away. (This is in the context of dating relationships only.)

When the relationship is in sexual sin. If you are in a relationship that is committing sexual immorality, you need to surrender it to God, unless you and your partner acknowledge your sin, come to repentance, and completely turn away from it. For many people that are in relationships where there is sexual sin, it is impossible to resist the temptation. They either don't know how to, or they simply don't want to. Only God can convict us of our sin and give us the self-control to crucify the desires of our flesh and say *no* to sexual immorality. If turning away from sexual sin is very difficult for you, then the best thing is to give that relationship to God and ask Him for power and self-control to abstain from sex until marriage.

When the Holy Spirit tells you to. Sorrow and sexual immorality don't necessarily have to be present in a relationship in order to know whether you should surrender it to God. There will be times when you simply know in your heart that God is asking you to give it up to Him. Sometimes the Holy Spirit is going to start making you feel uncomfortable one way or another. When that happens, it does not mean that you will stop having feelings for the other person; in fact, you may be very much in love and at the same time know that you have to let him go. This is because your flesh wants to continue with that person, but the Holy Spirit is telling you otherwise.

But when he, the Spirit of truth, comes,
he will guide you into all the truth. He will not
speak on his own; he will speak only what he

hears, and he will tell you what is yet to come.
(John 16:13 NIV)

The Holy Spirit fulfills several functions: He teaches us, guides us, counsels us, intercedes for us, and convicts us of sin. He will be your best guide when it comes to choosing a partner. He will show and confirm to you if the person you are looking forward to starting a relationship with comes from God; if not, He will direct you away from that relationship.

There are several ways in which the Holy Spirit can speak to you. The most reliable way is through the Bible, which is the Word of God; but the Holy Spirit can also speak to you through your parents, your pastors, or to you directly. It is important to always make sure that what other people are saying or what you believe the Holy Spirit is speaking to you does not contradict the Word of God.

Many believers know they have to turn away from a relationship, either because it is sinful, unequally yoked, or simply because God has asked them to. Here is where many of them fail to obey God. Only when we know and love God can we truly obey Him. *Evidence of spiritual maturity is that our love for God results in denying ourselves and surrendering everything we are, everything we want, and everything we hope for to Him even when it is very difficult or painful.* God is glorified when we willingly obey Him at all costs. Every time we surrender to Him, we grow spiritually; and every time we disobey, we slow down our spiritual growth and delay the blessings and the fulfillment of His promises.

If you are in a relationship or contemplating whether to start one, I would like to encourage you to pray for guidance and direction, and to ask God if that relationship is in His will for you. I am confident that it will not take very long before you know His answer. Walk boldly and fearlessly in the instruction and path that God is laying down for you even if that means surrendering what you cherish and desire the most. You will not be disappointed. After some time of patient endurance, you will receive all that He has promised (Heb. 10:35–36).

CHAPTER 3

PRAYING FOR YOUR
FUTURE HUSBAND

As a single woman, I tried so many things in order to find love, but none of them worked. Instead of making things better, I usually found ways to actually make them worse. After various failed attempts, I finally came to the understanding that nothing that I could do would work if I was not constantly praying for my future husband. Praying for your future husband (even if you don't know him yet) will be your most powerful tool in obtaining the blessing that you are waiting for.

The way God works is very different from the way of the world. If you follow the patterns of this world to find a partner, you are more likely to dress with provocative clothing to get attention, hide your vulnerability, have sex before marriage, think it is acceptable to live with your boyfriend, follow your heart's desires, and not listen to the sound advice of your parents or the guidance of the scriptures. That is the formula for disaster. If you follow it, you may never find true love. You may, however, find yourself frustrated, exhausted, and heartbroken.

God's style is very different. The key to obtaining God's blessings is through prayer.

The Bible says:

> Keep on *asking*, and you will receive what
> you ask for. Keep on *seeking*, and you will find.

Keep on *knocking,* and the door will be opened to you. For everyone who asks, receives. Everyone who seeks, finds. And to everyone who knocks, the door will be opened . . . So if you sinful people know how to give good gifts to your children, how much more will your heavenly Father give good gifts to those who ask him. (Matt. 7:7–8, 11; NLT)

The above scripture talks about three things that should be done while you pray: *asking, seeking,* and *knocking. Ask* God for what you need as if you were lost in the desert and asking for water; *seek* with desperation as one who must find an answer; and *knock* as the one who will not give up on entering the room. As you seek God in prayer, He will work on your behalf and will manifest His glory in your life. Amazing things will happen!

Prayer consists of not only speaking to God but also hearing from Him. The main purpose of prayer is developing a relationship with Him. As we focus on God, He responds to us, revealing things to our spirits that otherwise we would never be able to know or understand.

Do you want to understand God's timing for the things for which you are waiting? Do you want to know what you need to do or stop doing in order to receive God's promises? Do you want to obtain wisdom in order to make the best decisions? If your answer is *yes* to any or all of these questions, then pray, pray, and pray some more! All the answers to these things and more, God can reveal to you in prayer. The Bible says that when we call to Him, He will answer, and He will reveal to us mysteries that we don't know (Jer. 33:3).

Prayer gives revelation

However, as it is written: "What no eye has seen, what no ear has heard, and what no human mind has conceived"—the things God has prepared for those who love him—*these are the things*

God has revealed to us by his Spirit. The Spirit searches all things, even the deep things of God. (1 Cor. 2:9–10, NIV)

The things that God has prepared for us go far beyond anything that we can imagine, yearn for, or desire. The longings of our heart are often finite compared to the destiny and plans that God has in store for us, which are eternal and full of His glory and greatness. Some of these things are mysteries that God wants to reveal to us, and it is only through prayer and having a close relationship with Him that those revelations will be given to us.

The Bible tells us that God will reveal to us things that are *confined* and *hidden* through His Holy Spirit (Jer. 33:3). We must immerse ourselves in the Word of God and in the presence of the Holy Spirit through prayer so that we can see, hear, feel, and discern the things that God is doing. If we do not spend time with the Holy Spirit and we don't build a relationship with God, we will never be able to walk in the destiny to which He has called us.

Just as in the natural, we have five senses (seeing, hearing, touching, smelling, and tasting); so in the spiritual, we have spiritual senses to see, hear, and feel spiritual things. Sometimes, God will give us a vision about things that are to come; other times, God will speak to our spirit things we need to know; and in other occasions, God will give us discernment about situations and people that are coming our way and will tell us what to do about them.

The kind of revelation that God gives us cannot be understood with our logic or reasoning, nor with our natural senses, because as it is written:

> The person without the Spirit does not accept the things that come from the Spirit of God but considers them foolishness, and cannot understand them because they are discerned only through the Spirit. (1 Cor. 2:14, NIV)

In other words, the things from God that are revealed to us by His Holy Spirit can only be understood and discerned spiritually. They do not make any sense in the natural. They might actually seem crazy, absurd, or dangerous; but if they come from the Holy Spirit of God, they are powerful to give us victory and to release miracles in our lives.

Having this kind of revelation is extremely powerful for all kinds of circumstances. At the moment of making the most important decisions of your life, such as choosing whom you are going to marry, the Holy Spirit will be your most trusted Guide. If someone is pursuing you or comes and says to you, "You're the woman I've been looking for," God's Spirit will give you discernment about that person if you have been seeking His direction through prayer. You will be able to compare what God has revealed to you in the Spirit with what is coming your way. Therefore, you will be able to know whether that person or opportunity comes from God or not. If you are not sure, you should continue to pray until you receive complete confirmation and clear revelation.

— ♡♡ —

Teresa is a young woman who had been praying for a husband. She met a man who immediately began to pursue her. When Teresa first saw him, she actually thought that he was very good looking; he was tall, attractive, and had a charming smile. He seemed to be very interested in her from the beginning and told her that he wanted to keep getting to know her.

As they started to hang out and know each other more, he told her that he was a Christian and that he had been praying for a wife. "I believe that you are the woman for whom I have been praying," he said. However, for some strange reason, Teresa started to feel very uncomfortable around him. There was something about him that didn't feel right, and she did not know what it was. After all, he was kind, attentive, and good looking. What could possibly be wrong?

Teresa continued to pray and said to God, "Lord, if this man does not come from you, please take him away from me. I do not want to waste my time if you did not send him." She remembered that the Word of God says, "Trust in the Lord with all your heart and lean not on your own understanding; in all your ways submit to him, and he will make your paths straight" (Prov. 3:5–6, NIV)

The man continued to call her for weeks. However, the more he called her, the more uncomfortable she felt. She knew that she should not accept any other invitation from him again. She couldn't find a good reason for such a decision, other than her intuition that something about him was not right.

Days later, Teresa received a call from a woman she did not know. The woman said, "Hi, I'm calling you because I just saw on my husband's phone that he has been calling and texting you. I'm his wife. I just called to find out; who are you?" Teresa was shocked! Fortunately, she had decided not to see that man anymore because her heart was attuned to the leadership of the Holy Spirit.

— 💕 —

The rest of the conversation is history. The point is that God revealed the true intentions and the deceitful heart of that man. That discomfort Teresa felt from the beginning was the Holy Spirit giving her discernment, warning her that she was in danger and that man couldn't be trusted. Teresa did well to keep on praying and waiting for God to reveal what was going on. The Bible says that we shouldn't make any judgments about anyone ahead of time for the Lord will bring the private motives and darkest secrets of people to light (1 Cor. 4:5, NLT).

Being in tune with the Holy Spirit will give you clarity and direction. It will keep you from making terrible mistakes! Therefore, be alert and guard your heart; pray without ceasing for your future husband, for wisdom, and discernment to not be deceived so you will not end up falling in love with the wrong person.

How shall we pray?

Prayer is not engrained in our fleshly nature; we all need to learn how to pray. Jesus's instruction was to go into our room, close the door, and pray to our Heavenly Father in private (Matt. 6:6). Three aspects of effective prayer are:

1. to pray according to God's will;
2. to believe that whatever we ask in prayer, we will receive; and
3. to pray in Jesus's name.

Praying according to His will.

> This is the confidence we have in approaching God: that if we ask anything *according to his will*, he hears us. And if we know that he hears us—whatever we ask—we know that we have what we asked of him. (1 John 5:14–15, NIV)

There is a condition for God to hear and answer our prayers: that we pray according to His will. While God responds to all of our prayers, many times, that response is no because we are not praying in accordance to His will.

We can spend a lot of time praying for something and not seeing an answer because we are not praying as we should. It is possible that we are not praying according to God's will even when it seems like what we are asking for is a good thing.

— ♡ —

Selene prayed for years about her husband. In her prayers, she asked for things that seemed good to her: a man who was no more than five years older than her, who was actively involved in ministry, and who worked in the medical field because she was a nurse. She also prayed for several physical characteristics. Her list was quite detailed and specific. She was constantly rejecting any man who did not meet her criteria. She was not willing to accept anything less than what she had prayed for.

Over the years, she met very few guys with the looks and requirements she had been praying for. Whenever she met some-one that was close enough to the description in her prayer list, she immediately thought, "This is the one!" However, as soon as she started a relationship, she had great disappointments over and over again. Some guys were cocky, others very immature, others very full of themselves, others not ready for commitment.

One day, Selene met Gabriel, a guy who did not meet the exten-sive list of characteristics for which she had been praying. Gabriel liked Selene, but Selene was so focused on what she wanted that she paid no attention to him. Gabriel was faithful to God and had been praying for years for a godly wife. He had a humble heart, was responsible, hardworking, and respectful. Gabriel attended church but was not involved in any ministry. When Gabriel met Selene, he thought that Selene was the woman he had been praying for. He sub-tly started to pursue her, but she gave him the cold treatment since he didn't meet her protocol.

Little by little, he started to get her attention. Selene noticed there were things about him that she really liked—he made her feel special, beautiful, and cherished. They always had tons of fun together and interesting conversations. Selene finally began to pray for God to reveal His will about Gabriel. She felt in her spirit that God said to her:

"For a long time, you have been praying for what you want, but My plans are better than yours. You have been so focused praying for your desired list of qualities. However, you have overlooked the most important aspect—knowing the heart of the other person. Gabriel is a man after my own heart."

When Selene received this revelation, she repented for having been praying according to what she selfishly wanted and not accord-ing to the will of God. Her lack of humility had become a major obstacle for her to recognize the blessing that God was putting before her eyes. She finally knew that Gabriel was the man that her heart longed for. Once she accepted the invitation to become his girlfriend, she was able to fully appreciate him for who he was, a treasure from heaven. They complemented each other perfectly, and soon after they started dating, they got married.

Today she sighs and says, "God went beyond what I had ever dreamed or imagined I would find in a husband."

—— ♡ ——

God will not always give us what we want, but He will always give us what we need, what He knows is best for us.

Selene received discernment from the Holy Spirit to understand that Gabriel was indeed a blessing from God. If she had not prayed and been sensitive to hear the voice of the Holy Spirit, she might still be single, having disappointment after disappointment.

You may wonder, "How do I know if I am praying according to God's will?" In reality, it takes time and practice. Nobody is born knowing how to pray according to the will of God. The most effective way is by knowing His will, which we can find in the Bible. However, we also have a helper, the Holy Spirit. If we ask the Holy Spirit to help us pray, He will guide us in our prayer.

> In the same way, *the Spirit helps us* in our weakness. We do not know what we ought to pray for, but *the Spirit himself intercedes for us* through wordless groans. (Rom. 8:26, NIV)

When you pray for your husband, ask the Holy Spirit to help you pray according to the will of God. You can say, "Lord, you know that I want a man like this, but not my will, but yours be done." This is *surrender*, remember? When you pray this way, God is pleased with your humility since you are acknowledging that you don't have the wisdom to know what is best for you, but He does. Maybe you will need to give up certain expectations you have about the man of your dreams. Allow God to put His dreams in you instead. As I explained in the previous chapter, sooner or later, you need to surrender your desire for love to God if you want to receive His best.

Believing and not doubting in prayer.

> Therefore I tell you, whatever you ask for in prayer, *believe* that you have received it, and it will be yours. (Mark 11:24, NIV)

There may be so many circumstances that you are facing that make you think God cannot bring the husband that you have been praying for. Let me share my own personal experience to illustrate this with an example. When I was single, I worked from home for seven years for a foreign company. I spent hours sitting at a desk in front of a computer without having any contact with the outside world until I finished my workday. Some days, I saw the sunrise and the sunset while still working at the same desk.

My job was very demanding and isolating. My office was my bedroom, a tiny room with a small bed, a closet, a corner desk, and a chair. At that time, I was living with my family, rarely spending time with others or meeting new people. I had a few friends from church, which was a small congregation. I hung out with the same circle of church friends for almost seven years. In the evenings after I finished working, I attended a gymnastics class in which I was the oldest gymnast; all the kids were under sixteen while I was twenty-eight. And that was it. That was my life in a nutshell and the extent of the social interaction that I had. Not a very ideal scenario for meeting prince charming, right?

All of these factors and unique circumstances made me wonder many times how I could ever possibly meet the man who would be my husband. I wondered how God would bring him into my life. "Will He send him to knock right at my door one day?" I joked hopelessly. It really required a miracle! I had no idea how God was going to do it.

Today, I can understand that all those years when I felt so alone and isolated were in fact years of preparation during which God tested and perfected my trust in Him. God had me right there, in that place and in that situation, for a purpose. In the end, my particular circumstances were not any kind of obstacle that the God of the universe could not get around in order to bless me with my husband. They were, in fact, something that God used completely in my favor in order to prepare me to receive His promise.

Sometimes our finite minds are so limited that we can only see our circumstances, but we are unable to understand that God has infinite resources to carry out His plan. God was faithful and brought my husband into my life despite all the circumstances that were against me. Later in this book, I will tell you how He did it.

If you have been waiting on God for a husband and you have been faithful to Him and walking in obedience, be confident that He will fulfill His promise. If you have been praying for a husband, believe that in His perfect time, God will bring him into your life. Maybe you feel discouraged thinking that your circumstances are obstacles that will stop you from receiving the blessing of God. Maybe your age, the place where you live, your job, or the fact that you don't know many people is causing your heart to worry. All of these things can bring doubt and fear as to whether God can do the work or not. Recall that when God promised Abraham a son, despite the fact that he was a one-hundred-year-old man and his wife Sarah was a barren woman, he obtained the promise because *he believed and did not doubt* that God had the power to do what He had promised (Rom. 4:20–21).

The key is to *believe* in spite of the circumstances. "'If you can?' said Jesus. 'Everything is possible for one who believes.'" (Mark 9:23, NIV). We must not lose heart, we must not lose faith, we should not put our eyes on the giants that are coming our way, but on God. God is not limited by our circumstances; the only ones who can put a limit on what God can do is us. Our faith and our prayers are like fuel that God uses to manifest His power and glory in our lives. How can we recognize that God has done something for us if we have never asked Him in the first place? Rather, our faith is strengthened when we receive what we have asked for in prayer.

> Do not be anxious about anything, but in every situation, by prayer and petition, with thanksgiving, present your requests to God. And the peace of God, which transcends all understanding, will guard your hearts and your minds in Christ Jesus. (Phil. 4:6–7, NIV)

For many women, it is difficult to wait for a long time to find love without feeling anxious about it. I know that there are women who do not experience any anxiety on this matter; however, I have not had the pleasure to meet one yet. It is normal to experience anxiety and distress sometimes in our life; what is not normal is to be anxious about something all the time. The Bible tells us that we should not worry or be anxious about anything, but rather we should pray for everything, including the matter that causes us anxiety. If you have been going through a time of anguish, worried because you don't know whether or not you will one day get married, prayer will bring incredible relief. When you pray and you place your petitions in the hands of God with genuine faith, you can experience peace and rest, trusting that He will take control.

Sometimes God does not fight our battles until we stop trying to fight them ourselves. We cannot expect God to give us a godly husband when we go to the wrong places to find a partner. We cannot expect to receive from God a man who respects us when we engage in sex outside of marriage or when we allow someone to caress us inappropriately. We cannot expect to receive a man who strives to conquer our heart when we are the ones that go after him. If you are praying for a godly husband, then stay firm in your walk with God, do not deviate from His will, act and live a life according to what you are asking for.

> But when you ask, you must believe and not doubt, because the one who doubts is like a wave of the sea, blown and tossed by the wind. That person should not expect to receive anything

from the Lord. Such a person is double-minded
and unstable in all they do. (James 1:6–8, NIV)

A woman that is unstable in her faith is double-minded:

- One day she believes that God will do it, and the next day she is not sure anymore.
- She prays for a man that is fully committed to her, but she doesn't guard her heart and gives it to one man after another.
- She prays for a godly husband, but she goes out and looks for a partner in the wrong places (such as bars and nightclubs).
- She ends a relationship that was in sexual sin, and after a week, she wants to come back to it.

Do you get the idea?

Don't be tossed around like sea waves. We must ask in faith and not doubt that God has all the power and all the resources to bring the answer.

Praying in the name of Jesus.

> And I (Jesus) will do whatever you ask in
> my name, so that the Father may be glorified
> in the Son. You may ask me for anything in my
> name, and I will do it. (John 14:13–14, NIV)

This is perhaps the most important aspect of prayer: that whatever we ask for, we do it in the name of Jesus. This is a basic and important principle of prayer that may be obvious to many believers; however, many people do not know about it, and I consider it essential. In the name of Jesus, there is power. Jesus said that all power and authority have been given to Him in heaven and on earth (Matt. 28:18). When you pray, always close your prayer with, "I pray/ask these things in the name of Jesus. Amen."

I hope this chapter has helped you understand how important and powerful prayer for your future husband is and how you should pray. The main purpose of prayer is not so much receiving something from God, but listening to His voice and developing a relationship with Him. His answer to our requests comes as a result of us calling to Him and also of walking obediently as we listen to the instruction that He is giving us.

It is possible that you have been praying for a long time, maybe a few months, or even a few years, without seeing any answer yet. You have not met your husband, you are still single, and nothing appears to have changed; so what's going on? In the next chapter, I will explain why sometimes, God's answer seems delayed. There may be spiritual hindrances, or God may first want to accomplish something in you or your future husband before you are introduced. I want to reassure you; your prayers are not in vain. When you pray, God is working on your behalf.

CHAPTER 4

WHEN GOD'S ANSWER SEEMS TO BE DELAYED

We often expect God to respond to our prayers in our timing. I don't want to discourage you, but it rarely happens that way. Just as we can have a prayer answered instantly, it can also take months or even years before we see God's answer especially when we are praying for a spouse. This is when many singles stop persevering in prayer, and they give up. This is a big mistake. The only time we should stop praying is when we have received what we have been praying for.

Even if time goes by and we don't see an answer to our prayers, that doesn't mean that nothing is happening. We might think that God has not heard us or that our prayer is not being answered. However, God never sleeps; He is always working on our behalf. It sometimes *seems* that His answer to our prayers is not coming, but do not give up. Your *endurance* is making you a mature person in faith (James 1:3–4), preparing you to receive everything He has in store for you.

Before God blessed me with my husband, I spent years praying for him, asking God to prepare him for me. The time came when I felt I was ready to receive this blessing, and God's answer still had not arrived. As years went by, I started to get discouraged. I asked God why it was taking Him so long to bless me with a spouse. Nothing was happening in my life that made me think God's answer to my prayer was on the way; at least nothing that my eyes could see. But behind the scenes, God was aligning things and opening the way to introduce me to the love of my life.

I finally came to the realization of how God used my prayers the day my husband-to-be proposed to me. He went down on one knee, asked me to be his wife, and after I said *yes,* he looked into my eyes and said, "Wow, I'm so amazed at God. His timing is perfect! He brought you into my life right when I was ready, not before or after." His response perplexed me.

"Why do you think you weren't ready before?" I said.

Then he responded, "If I had known you two years ago, I would have ruined this relationship. I was not the man that I am today, the man that you need as a husband. God was working on my faith and character. He was giving me direction. And when I was finally ready, He brought you to me."

I was shocked! That was a very revealing moment for me. At last, I knew the reason why God was taking so long! While I was anguished for years, crying on my knees, thinking that God had not listened to my prayers, many things were actually happening. I just wasn't able to see them. Even though I thought I was ready for marriage, I wasn't, and my husband wasn't either. God used our prayer in a powerful way to prepare us for each other.

God was making a way ahead of us, to bless us with the spouse that each of us needed. During the waiting time, He was preparing our hearts and strengthening our faith so that we might have the marriage that we have today—a strong, Christ-centered, happy, and healthy marriage.

Why is it taking so long?

If you have been praying for a husband and you have not yet received an answer, most likely you are wondering, "Has God heard my prayers?" I wondered this many times. Just imagine, from the moment I started praying for a husband until the moment that God brought him into my life was seven years! I don't want you to get worried about what your timing might be. God has very different times for each of us, and His timing is perfect. However, if you have ever doubted whether God has heard your prayers, the answer is this: if you have been praying according to His will, from the first day you began to pray, your prayer was not only *heard,* it was also *answered.*

Many times, God has already responded to our prayers, but we haven't received the answer yet. There is something that can hinder our prayers or delay the response to them called *spiritual opposition.*

Spiritual opposition. For anything you pray, there is spiritual opposition that can delay the answer to your prayers. *Spiritual opposition* is a battle between good and evil; the *resistance* that Satan will bring against the work of God. This battle takes place in the spiritual realm, an invisible world that we cannot see with our natural eyes but can only be perceived with our spiritual senses. In this place, there is ongoing warfare that affects our lives every day.

If our spiritual eyes were opened so that we could see what is happening in this realm, we would probably be paralyzed and in shock. We would see angels and demons fighting battles all the time and other unthinkable things! Perhaps God does not allow us to see this realm on a daily basis in order to protect us, since we aren't ready to understand all these things. Sometimes, God does give us a glimpse into this realm when He wants to reveal something to us for His purposes.

Daniel, a man who was highly esteemed by God, prayed and fasted for the restoration of the city of Jerusalem, which had been reduced to rubble during the Babylonian captivity. After praying and fasting for a long time, Daniel started to wonder why his prayers had not been answered. Unbeknownst to him, his prayer had been hindered by spiritual opposition. An angel appeared to Daniel and said:

> Do not be afraid, Daniel. Since the first day
> that you set your mind to gain understanding and
> to humble yourself before your God, your words
> were *heard,* and I have come in *response* to them.
> But the prince of the Persian kingdom *resisted* me
> twenty-one days. (Dan. 10:12–13, NIV)

The angel Gabriel comforts Daniel, telling him that his prayer was *heard* and *answered* from the first day that Daniel prayed. And why hadn't he received that answer? Because the Prince of Persia had been *resisting* (fighting against) him. The Prince of Persia was not a physical person, but a demonic principality sent by Satan to stop the angel that was coming in response to Daniel's prayer. In other words, the Prince of Persia was a *spiritual opposition.*

Daniel received an answer to his prayer much later than what he had anticipated. What Daniel perceived as a *delayed* response from God, in reality, was an answered prayer *hindered* by opposition. We will also face spiritual opposition against anything that we are praying for. Although the warfare is happening in the spiritual realm, we are sometimes able to feel its effects in our spirit as feelings of being distressed, burdened, worn out, or restless come over us.

The spiritual opposition that you might experience in the realm of love might come in the form of:

- *intrusive thoughts* such as fear, depression, doubts, insecurities, anxiety, and low self-esteem;
- *unresolved issues from your past* such as betrayal, infidelity, emotional wounds, resentment, past trauma, and physical or verbal abuse;
- *sins and temptations* such as premarital sex, substance abuse (alcohol, drugs), pornography, arrogance, and pride.

Do any of the above sound familiar? These might be some of the spiritual hindrances the enemy will use against you in your quest for love, but there are many more. The only way we can win spiritual battles and overcome spiritual opposition is through prayer. We cannot win these battles ourselves. Only Jesus can set us free from any spiritual bondage and sin affecting our souls. We need to truly repent from our sins and ask for deliverance from anything that is hindering our progress.

Prayer brings salvation and deliverance

God uses our prayers to work in us and through us to bless other people. Your prayers have power to bring salvation, restoration, and deliverance to the man that will be your husband.

Let's take a look at Adriana and Hector's story.

—— ♡ ——

Adriana had been a Christian all her life. She had several relationships, some long term and some short term. Over and over again, she had great disappointments and heartbreaks. Despite feeling discouraged, she continued to pray and decided to guard her heart and not to give it away to anyone until she was convinced that she was in the presence of her future husband, brought to her by God's own hand.

When Adriana first met Hector, she never imagined that they would be married one day. Hector had lived separated from God all his life. He had had multiple sexual relationships with women; he had been a drug addict too. Hector had been attending Adriana's church for a few months. He was invited by a friend, and after that invitation, he continued to attend every Sunday. Although Hector was not a Christian, his mother was, and she constantly prayed for her son to know the Lord and give up his life to Him. As Hector started to attend church, the Lord began a transformation in him, changing his heart. Hector turned away from his past and repented from all of his sins. God delivered him from his alcohol abuse and drug problems.

Eventually, Adriana and Hector became friends and were attending the same Bible-study group for single adults. It must have taken a great leap of faith for Adriana to trust God when He revealed to her that Hector was going to be her husband. After a year of knowing each other, they decided to start a formal relationship; and before another year went by, they were married.

Today, Hector is a man who has been completely transformed by God. He is a loving husband and an excellent father. He is a testimony of what God can do in the heart of a person who walks apart from God all of his life and then fully surrenders himself to Christ.

After hearing Hector's story and seeing the transformation that God did in him, Adriana understood that all those years that she had been praying for a husband, God was working in Hector's life. God was very busy orchestrating the moment in which Hector would have a personal encounter with the transformational and unconditional love of Christ and be saved.

———— ♡ ————

God wanted Hector to have an opportunity to repent and be rescued by Him. Adriana's prayers for her future husband accomplished this and more. God knew that Hector was not ready to receive the blessing of a woman like Adriana, but He also knew that Hector had the potential to become the blessing for which Adriana had been praying. God sees far beyond our present circumstances and our shortcomings. He is not limited by our mistakes. He sees who we are in Christ: "More than conquerors through Him," (Rom. 8:37). In other words, He sees the best version of ourselves and our full potential in Jesus Christ.

> The Lord isn't really being slow about his promise, as some people think. No, he is being patient for your sake. He does not want anyone to be destroyed, but wants everyone to repent.
> (2 Pet. 3:9, NLT)

Adriana always thought that the man who would be her husband was going to be a lifelong Christian just as she was, but that was not the case. God instead gave her a man He transformed into someone who was ready to be the husband she needed. We will never know what God's ways and plans are; He has no molds or protocols. *God does not necessarily choose the most qualified, but He always qualifies the ones that He chooses.*

While we pray, God is working in us and for us even when we cannot track what He is doing. If you have been praying for a husband and God has not brought him into your life yet, it is surely because God is working in both of you. You may already feel ready, but the truth is that God is teaching both of you to trust Him, and He knows the perfect time to introduce you!

Ask the Holy Spirit to show you what kind of hindrances or opposition might be delaying the answer to your prayers. There might be things from your past such as hurts and disappointments that have wounded you and that are stopping you from moving forward. It could also be that your husband-to-be needs deliverance in some areas of his life and even to receive salvation! Pray for yourself and for your future husband, ask God to prepare both of you for each other.

When you pray according to the will of God and with faith, you can be sure that from the first day you prayed, your prayer was heard; and if it was heard, you can trust that God will answer it. This is the promise He has given us in the Bible, and God does not fail. Even if the answer takes a while, you should not hesitate nor stop praying. The man who is going to be your husband needs your prayers at all times. He needs them before you even know him, and he will need them even more once you become his wife.

If you have been praying for a husband for a long time, do not give up but persevere. Your prayers are being used in a powerful way; you just cannot see it yet. You may be surprised one day when God reveals to you all He was doing in you and in your future partner while you were praying. So do not get discouraged for from the first day you humbled your heart before God and started praying for a husband, your prayer was not only *heard*, it was also *answered*. And the answer is coming your way.

CHAPTER 5

OVERCOMING THE FEARS
OF LOVE AND DATING

One of the biggest obstacles for many single people who wish to succeed in love is fear. Many people destroy their relationships or run away from them because they have not been able to overcome the fears and traumas of their past. The common response of man toward fear is to flee from what seems threatening even if the apparent threat is only imagined. Fear is contrary to faith in God. It causes us to believe that something bad is going to happen, and speaking our fears aloud can give life to the things we fear the most.

Most fears have their root in something that happened to us in the past. If you have been hurt before, you might fear you will be hurt again. If you were rejected or someone cheated on you, then you might become very cautious about future relationships, thinking that the same scenario will be repeated.

Fear makes us insecure and cautious; it makes us wonder if we have what it takes to be loved and accepted. This is why fear sometimes causes people to become possessive, overly jealous, demanding, and unable to trust, slowly suffocating their relationships until they destroy them.

Have you ever filtered your relationships based on the following thinking processes?

- You do not want to make the same mistakes your parents made.
- You do not want to be hurt like the last time you opened your heart.
- You just feel that you are not worthy of love.
- You think you need to play hard to get.
- You don't want anybody to take advantage of you.
- You don't want to be vulnerable, showing your true emotions and feelings.

All of the above thoughts are rooted in fear; they are all linked to past disappointments, hurt, and pain. Fear prevents us from being free to experience and receive the love that we truly deserve and want.

There were several instances when I approached relationships very cautiously especially if I felt very attracted to the other person. Past relationships had taught me that when I felt very attracted to somebody, I normally ended up more emotionally invested than the other person. The other person in turn took advantage of the situation and acted like a jerk. Because of that, my mechanism of defense was to hide my emotions and feelings, and to play hard to get. I wasn't myself; I was the person who I thought the other person would feel attracted to. Although this approach seemed to work temporarily, it wasn't sustainable long term. Those relationships became very superficial, shallow, unreal, calculated, emotionally consuming; and they never lasted.

As believers, we have not been called to live in fear but rather in the freedom that can only be experienced through complete trust in God. Trusting in God allows us to face the future confidently and sets us free from the wounds and traumas of our past.

God knows that during the course of our lives, fear inevitably is going to assault us in different ways. It is easy to experience fear because of various circumstances that seem threatening. Yet God's instruction has always been this: fear not.

> Don't be afraid, for I am with you. Don't be
> discouraged, for I am your God. I will strengthen

you and help you. I will hold you up with my victorious right hand. (Isa. 41:10, NLT)

As you can see in the above scripture, "the antidote to the emotion of fear is the conviction that God is for us and with us."[7]

There are three steps to overcoming fear:

Step 1: *Identification*—what am I afraid of?
Step 2: *Knowing its source*—what caused this fear?
Step 3: *Confrontation*—what does the Word of God say that helps me overcome this fear?

The only way to overcome our fears is by *confronting* them, which means to continue moving forward courageously in spite of them. Eventually, fear will submit to your courage; it will lose its power and will become a thing of the past.

Top fears of love and dating

When it comes to love and dating, there are so many fears that haunt singles. In this section, I will talk about five major fears of love and dating. For each of them, I will apply the three steps to overcome fear.

Fear of loneliness.

Identification: Fear of being alone and not having anyone by your side.

Being single is good, God created singleness with a good purpose. Even when you desire to find a man who loves you and get married one day, you should not allow that desire to take away the joy of singleness or make you feel anxious about it.

---

7   Richards, Lawrence O. *New International Encyclopedia of Bible Words* (Grand Rapids, MI: Zondervan, 1991), p. 272

The fear of loneliness is not the same as feeling lonely. Loneliness is a fact of life. We will be alone several times throughout the course of our lives, but we shouldn't be afraid of it. A key sign of the *fear of loneliness* is when a person cannot stay single for a long period of time. She is always looking to find her emotional, physical, or financial fulfillment in another person. As soon as she breaks up with one relationship, she is already looking for someone else to date. Some people afraid of being alone would even prefer to stay in abusive and unloving relationships rather than just being single.

Source: The underlying cause of this fear is the false assumption that you need someone else to take care of you. If you take care of yourself emotionally, spiritually, financially, and physically, you most likely will not have fear of being alone.

Confrontation:

> Not that I speak from [any personal] need,
> for I have learned to be *content* [and *self-sufficient*
> through Christ, *satisfied* to the point where I am
> *not disturbed* or uneasy] regardless of my circum-
> stances. (Phil. 4:11, AMP)

The apostle Paul learned to be *self-sufficient* in Christ's suffi-ciency. As believers, we must find contentment and satisfaction in Christ alone. We must accept with joy and gratitude whatever stage of life God has us in, whether we are single or married. He has us there for a period of time to fulfill a purpose. We must be able to find our fulfillment and contentment in God long before He gives us a husband. In fact, being fulfilled in God alone is a great sign of maturity that indicates that one is getting ready to receive the bless-ing of marriage.

Even if God has not yet brought a partner to your life, Jesus is and will always be your husband. In Him, you will find strength for every circumstance that you are going through. If God said, "It is not good for man to be alone," it is because He knows our need for love and companionship. When He considers it appropriate and sees fit for you to have a husband, He will fulfill this longing of your heart.

Fear of not being worthy of love (fear of rejection).

Identification: Fear of no one loving you because you feel that you don't deserve it.

The fear of not being worthy of love is very subtle, sometimes unperceivable to the person. Key signs of having this fear are low self-esteem, being insecure and feeling nervous toward people of the opposite sex that we feel attracted to.

Source: Rejection.

This fear has its origin in rejection. Perhaps you have experienced some degree of rejection since you were young. For example, if your parents made you feel that you did not live up to their standards of cleanliness, discipline, or performance in certain areas of your life, you might have felt rejected. Statements such as, "You are good for nothing," "You always do things wrong," "You disappoint me," "You will never accomplish anything," begin to sow small seeds of rejection into your heart. The fruit of those seeds is fear of failure, of not being accepted, or of being taken advantaged.

This fear could also be the result of painful experiences with past love relationships. I had to overcome this fear myself. The disappointment of several relationships made me think that there was something wrong with me, that I was not good enough and that I had to try harder.

Any kind of verbal, physical, emotional, and mental abuse can be highly destructive. Our emotional wounds from the past take time to heal, and it is only Jesus who can free us from the pain that other people caused us. As Jesus's love begins to heal you, it will be possible for you to gain confidence in yourself and to discover your true worth as a person.

Confrontation:

And may you have the power to understand, as all God's people should, how wide, how long, how high, and how deep his love is. May you experience the love of Christ, though it is too great to understand fully. Then you will be *made*

complete with all the fullness of life and power
that comes from God. (Eph. 3:18–19, NLT)

Understanding how precious you are to God and how great
His love is for you is the first step toward being delivered from the
fear of feeling unworthy of love. God's love will make you a *complete*
person, not needing anyone's attention or approval. We all want to
be accepted and loved, but that will not always happen. Jesus himself
was humiliated and rejected by men for no reason. But he did not
come to please men, but to do the will of His Father. You might also
find that by doing the will of God, some people might reject you,
and that is perfectly wonderful.

Maybe some men who were initially interested in you will be
turned off when you do not accept having sex until marriage. Maybe
they will not feel attracted to you anymore when they find out about
your faith and your Christian values. But do not be discouraged, *you
do not need* any of these men. God will remove everything and everyone that hinders your faith and your walk with Him. Sooner or later,
God will reward your obedience and faithfulness with a man who is
able to see your worth for who you are, a woman of God.

Fear of being hurt (again).

Identification: Fear of someone hurting your feelings or taking
advantage of you.

When we have been hurt, we tend to build an emotional shield
of protection, we hide our true emotions and feelings, we become
reserved about verbalizing thoughts, we avoid being vulnerable and
sharing details of our life, we hide our true selves. The problem comes
when our position of self-protection prevents us from being able to
form genuine love relationships based on trust and honesty. If we
become calculating, unable to express or demonstrate feelings and
emotions assertively, or if we are overly suspicious and cautious, there
will not be any depth in the relationships we form with other people.

Source: Rejection, heartbreak, and past disappointments.

The fear of being hurt develops when we have experienced heartbreaks and rejection. This is especially true for people that have suffered a divorce, infidelity, or abandonment. The pain of past failed relationships leaves deep wounds in our souls that are difficult to heal or ignore. We are afraid of being hurt again, and in turn, we become overly cautious.

Confrontation:

> Nevertheless, I will bring health and healing to my people; I will heal them and will let them enjoy abundant peace and security. (Jer. 33:6, NIV)

God's love is the ultimate source of healing from any hurts from your past. It is important for you to know that God will not send you someone who will cause you suffering. If you really wait on the Lord and let Him choose your partner, you should not be afraid to be hurt again. For He has said that in Him, we will enjoy abundant peace and security.

Whatever your situation is, do not allow your mind and heart to dwell permanently on the deception of past failed relationships. Recovering from the pain and healing from the wounds of the past is a process that will take time. You must be ready for the Lord to heal you, restore you, and show you the new path that you should follow. Perhaps God wants you to set your focus completely on Him for now. God will restore what you have lost, He will do something new in you (Isa. 43:19), and He will deliver you from your pain.

Fear of commitment.

Identification: Fear of joining yourself with another person for the rest of your life.

Commitment and marriage are both decisions of faith. When you have fear of commitment or marriage, the first question you need to ask yourself is this: "Do I firmly believe that this is the partner that

God has for me?" If you hesitate in your response, then I completely understand why you are afraid. I would be freaking out too!

In the most important decision of your life—choosing the person with whom you will be united in marriage—you must be sure that God is guiding your steps. His direction will be revealed to you through His Word and through prayer. If you do not have the conviction that God is guiding you in this decision, do not rush. Wait a little bit longer until you are fully convinced about it. Pray for a sign, seek the advice of your parents, and make wise decisions. I guarantee you that when God reveals to you what to do, whether to marry that person or not, all fear will be gone.

Source: Lack of conviction or confirmation from God.

You might think there may be someone better out there than the person you are dating. This way of thinking is common when there is no conviction that God has joined you to this person. If this is your thinking, what is the point of continuing in that relationship? Do not waste your time, and do not waste the time of the other person. No one deserves to be somebody's secondhand rose. If you perceive that the person you are dating is thinking this way about you, let him go! Let him keep looking for what he has not found yet; you deserve someone who truly loves you.

Confrontation:

> For this reason a man will leave his father
> and mother and be united to his wife, and the
> two will become one flesh. (Eph. 5:31, NIV)

Marriage is God's design, it is a blessing, and it is a good thing. There is no reason to be afraid of marriage or commitment unless the decision of marrying has not been led by God. The Bible says that he (or she) who finds a wife (or husband) finds what is good and receives favor from the Lord (Prov. 18:22).

Perhaps your fear of marriage has a root that you need to identify. Did your parents have a broken marriage? Were you in an abusive relationship in the past? Were you previously engaged and the engagement was broken? All of these are examples of some traumas that can affect your perspective about commitment and marriage.

If there is a root to your fear and you can identify it, bring it to the feet of Jesus, ask the Holy Spirit to deliver you from such trauma and fear, and ask God to lead your steps to choose the right partner. As long as God is leading your steps and your decision to get married, you shouldn't be afraid.

Fear of committing the same mistakes (sins) as your parents.

Identification: Fear of repeating or following the mistakes of your parents.

When choosing who you are going to marry, your decision should be entirely led by the revelation and guidance of the Holy Spirit. You should not base your decision on your fears of what your parents did wrong or what your partner's parents did wrong.

Our parents can have a great impact, both positive and negative, on the way we conduct ourselves and on how we approach relationships. If we grew up in a family where our parents treated each other in a demeaning manner, or with anger, unforgiveness, dishonor, or physical or verbal abuse, it is possible that we might follow this same destructive model of behavior in our own marriage. The good news is that we can break these negative patterns of behavior.

Source: Past trauma, childhood abuse, parent's divorce, abandonment.

We live in a society ruled by dysfunctional marriages, and in which, divorce rates are increasing. There are many marital problems, including physical abuse, verbal abuse, infidelity, poverty, unforgiveness, poor communication, and anger, among others, which run rampant in our time. It is common to see these destructive patterns repeating themselves for several generations within the same family. The Bible calls these sins *iniquities* of the parents upon the children and grandchildren, and they can be repeated to the third and fourth generations (Exod. 34:7).

In *Marriage on the Rock Couple's Workbook,* author Jimmy Evans explains that, "The Hebrew word for *iniquities* is *avon,* which means a sin or problem created in you because of the same issue being modeled in your parent's family. Like a tree that is blown by the wind over and over, it becomes bent in the direction that it is blown, so a child is bent in the direction that he observes his parents."[8]

If you come from a dysfunctional family where the problems between your parents affected your childhood, it is very likely that you have developed certain fears about committing the same mistakes. However, these iniquities can be broken when people receive salvation through Christ, and God brings redemption and restoration (Deut. 5:9–10).

Confrontation:

> So if the Son sets you free, you will be free
> indeed. (John 8:36, NIV)

When you receive salvation through Christ, you also receive freedom! You should relinquish all fear about your past or the mistakes of your ancestors because if you are in Christ, the old is gone, and all things are new (2 Cor. 5:17).

To confront this fear, your thinking should be this: "My life will be different, my actions and my decisions will be different, and my marriage will be different. It will be a marriage of blessing because Jesus is my Lord and Savior, and He will be at the center of it."

Finally, you can pray and ask God to set you free from any iniquities from your ancestors:

> Lord Jesus, I pray that you break this iniquity off my life. I forgive my mother and father for their mistakes (sins) and what they did to me (or to each other). I bless my father and mother, and I ask you that in this moment, you set me free from committing the same mistakes (or sins) that my parents did.

---

[8]   Evans, Jimmy. *Marriage on the Rock Couple's Workbook* (Dallas, TX: Marriage Today™, 2014), p. 102

The iniquity should be broken in that moment! It is not your responsibility to carry the burdens of your parent's mistakes, neither to fix their problems nor to play the role of intermediary between them. The most effective thing you can do to help them is to pray for them and ask God to restore their relationship.

The source of all fears

> For God has not given us a spirit of fear and timidity, but of power, love, and self-discipline. (2 Tim. 1:7, NLT)

Fear does not come from God. God has given us His Holy Spirit, which enables us to carry out any task with courage, boldness, and power. Fear comes from Satan; he inspires lies in our mind. That's why he is called the father of lies (John 8:44). Satan wants us to believe that disastrous things are going to happen. He does this to paralyze us, preventing us from moving forward on the assignments and purposes of God.

Satan will constantly be inspiring negative thoughts in our minds such as:

- "Maybe God doesn't want me to get married."
- "God has not listened to my prayers."
- "I'll be alone forever."
- "I'm too old for finding love."
- "No one cares about me."
- "If I marry, my marriage will most certainly fail."
- "I am not enough."

His goal is to torment you and control your decisions. If you give enough power to your fears, you will end up believing Satan's lies and opening the door for the enemy to gain territory in your mind, emotions, and decisions.

There is only one way to overcome the devil and the fears that he inspires in us, and it is this: by resisting him!

> Submit yourselves, then, to God. *Resist the devil*, and he will flee from you. (James 4:7, NIV)

Resist the devil when he whispers thoughts of fear to your mind. You have been given a plan of action to overcome all your fears. Identify them, find the source, and then use the Word of God to confront them! Do not submit yourself to fear, but rather let fear submit to your courage as your spirit tells your flesh how things are going to be. Walk courageously, following the guidance of the Holy Spirit. Declare God's promises found in the Bible in your life. Sooner or later, you will cross paths with a man who loves you with the same kind of love that God loves you with—a love that casts out all fear (1 John 4:18).

CHAPTER 6

THE SPIRITS OF PRIDE AND INDEPENDENCE

The more that I spend time with single people, the more I see a pattern repeating itself. The most attractive, successful, and accomplished singles are usually the ones who have the hardest time finding love or maintaining successful relationships. It seems ironic that those who seem to have it all are precisely the ones who struggle the most to be fulfilled in their love lives. Look at the movie stars, actors, actresses, models, and celebrities; you will see this pattern I am talking about. Some of them, despite their fame, fortune, and physical attractiveness, remain unmarried for many years or a lifetime. Others that thought they finally found love get married, only to announce multi-million dollar divorces a few years later. Very few actually experience the fullness of love and succeed at staying in it. One day, while I was praying and meditating on this, God showed me the reason for this common pattern. A *spirit of pride* and a *spirit of independence* have been controlling the souls of many of these people.

The spirits of pride and independence are two unclean spirits that operate under the influence of Satan. Their sole purpose is to turn people away from God. People influenced by these spirits choose to do things themselves and follow their own will, not God's. These people are often arrogant and conceited; they consider themselves superior to others. They are also very prideful and think that

70

they can do everything on their own. The Lord showed me that pride and ungodly independence were keeping many people from receiving God's blessings, promises, and anointing.

People under the control of these two spirits are often unfulfilled in their love lives. They want to fall in love but are unable to find the right person. Even if the right person is in front of them, they cannot recognize them because pride has blinded their eyes and hardened their hearts. If these people do not identify the work these spirits are doing in their lives and break free from them, they can end up alone or in very unhealthy relationships.

The spirit of pride

A woman with a spirit of pride puts her trust in her abilities, possessions, accomplishments, looks, and intellect. This spirit goes hand in hand with *arrogance* and *conceit*. When a single woman has a spirit of pride and a man is pursuing her, she often rejects him, thinking that he is not good enough for her. She might perceive that he is not as successful or attractive as she desires. She might also feel superior in preparation, knowledge, skills, wealth, and even spirituality.

Pride and arrogance are evil in nature. They were the reason Satan was thrown out of paradise when he rebelled against God.

> Your heart became *proud* on account of your beauty, and you corrupted your wisdom because of your splendor. So I threw you to the earth; I made a spectacle of you before kings. (Ezek. 28:17 NIV)

Before his fall, Satan had a very exalted position in heaven's worship. It is believed that he led and orchestrated all the music in heaven. He was a beautiful angel, the model of perfection. He was full of wisdom and perfect in beauty. He was adorned with precious jewels and gold. However, his heart became *proud* due to his beauty. His splendor corrupted him. God expelled him from heaven because of the sin and wickedness found in him. And what was the root of his sin? Pride.

Unfortunately, in every one of us, there is pride. It is part of our sinful and fallen nature. God is not pleased with it because pride gives all credit to oneself instead of giving credit to God. *Pride loses sight of this: everything we are, we have, and we have accomplished is because of God and for His glory.* Without Him, we are nothing.

> This is what the Lord says: "Don't let the wise boast in their *wisdom*, or the powerful boast in their *power*, or the rich boast in their *riches*. But those who wish to boast should boast in this alone: That they truly know me and understand that I am the Lord." (Jer. 9:23–24, NLT)

The above scripture describes three things about which people feel pride: *wisdom*, what we know or have learned; *power*, our talents, skills, and our level of influence; and *wealth*, money or possessions we have. But God instructs us not to boast in any of these things for the only One who is worthy of all glory is He.

If you are a successful woman with many skills, knowledge, and talent, never forget that God has given you the ability to make wealth and to be successful because of His grace and for His glory. The blessing that He has put in your hands should never be a reason for pride, auto-exaltation, or arrogance, nor should they become your standard upon which you chose a partner.

> He did all this so you would never say to yourself, "I have achieved this wealth with my own strength and energy." Remember the Lord your God. He is the one who gives you power to be successful. (Deut. 8:17–18, NLT)

Pride can be so subtle that we do not even realize that it is controlling our lives. Only the light of God can reveal our sinful nature and allow us to see the pride in our hearts. I never realized how prideful I was until God brought me down from my self-made pedestal. For years, I had been a successful woman in my career. Everything I put my hand into prospered to such an extent that I gained recognition, fame, and wealth. I knew that God's favor was in my life, and I recognized that all I had accomplished was due to Him. But little by little, in a very subtle and silent manner, pride was growing its roots in my heart. Eventually, I started to see my success as the result of *my* skills and *my* talents, and forgot that God had given me the ability to be successful.

A time came when God allowed a long season of extreme illness in my life that lasted about three years. I was so weak physically, psychologically, and mentally. If I were to describe my state at that time with one word, it would be *handicapped*. I was handicapped in all aspects, unable to do anything that I was able to do before. All the strength, power, and skill I once boasted of were completely gone. But God allows everything for a reason, even the most unfortunate and painful events in our lives. In that season, He allowed me to see my vulnerability and limitations as a human. I was able to remember once again something I had forgotten: without Him and without His grace, I am nothing, and I am unable to do anything (John 15:5). Many times, the same blessings that God gives us are those that take us away from Him. Those blessings can make us proud if we fail to recognize from whom we have received them.

The Lord says:

> I took care of you in the wilderness, in that dry and thirsty land. But when you had eaten and were satisfied, you became proud and forgot me. (Hosea 13:5–6, NLT)

Listen to this carefully. I strongly believe that pride is getting in the way of many singles and is stopping them from taking hold of their love's blessing. Many people are remaining single because in their limited understanding of what they consider best for them, they have not found a person that fulfills their exhaustive list of standards. It is good to have standards. The question is: are your standards godly and divinely inspired, or are they based merely on your fleshly desires?

If your standards are to find a man of faith who is honest, who loves and respects you, who loves God, who is responsible, who protects you—all these things are standards based on the Word of God. If your standards are that he is over 6'2", has a good butt, is physically attractive, has a nice apartment, is rich, is of a specific skin color or nationality, then your standards are based on the desires of your flesh. God can bless you with a man who meets all of your fleshly desires, but they should not be your standard for choosing a partner. In my experience, most women and men who choose a partner based purely on their fleshly desires choose wrongly and are greatly disappointed along the road. Only God can change your expectations and guide you to choose the right person according to His Word; and this is the most reliable standard upon which to base your decisions.

The spirit of independence

The spirit of independence (ungodly independence) has nothing to do with your ability to support yourself, have your own apartment, or pay off all your debts. It is living a life independent from God and from the authority that He has established over you. A woman with a spirit of independence leads her own life and does not submit to anyone's authority. She likes to do things her way as she pursues her personal goals and interests. If she is single, she does not hold herself accountable to her parents. If she is married, she has problems submitting to the authority of her husband. She is a person who simply doesn't see anyone as her authority because she is her own authority.

Ungodly independence separates us from God and keeps us from fulfilling His plans and purposes. Yet Satan promotes ungodly independence as an attractive attribute in our current society. Some women become so independent that they find it very difficult or almost impossible to submit to anyone's authority. They think to themselves, "I have done things by myself all my life. I do not need anyone to tell me what to do or how to do it."

Some single men are attracted to women who project themselves as independent. Other men, with more conservative preferences, feel intimidated by women like these because they may seem unapproachable.

I asked some men what they think when they meet a woman who projects herself as very independent (with no authority over her). Here's what they said.

> When I see a woman like that, I wonder how she truly is. She projects herself as strong, self-sufficient, and confident, but will she be as inaccessible, calculating, self-focused, as she seems? Or will she be friendly, kind, and open to meeting someone like me?"
>
> —Thomas, age 35

> Sometimes I think that a woman who is too independent feels that she does not need a man. Well, at least that's what they project. So we [men] turn away from her. We like to feel that they need us and that we can provide protection.
>
> —Jim, age 41

> A woman who has her ways very established and her eyes fixed on her personal goals may not coincide with the ways and the goals of a man who is pursuing her. The question is how willing is she to compromise her goals in order to form a relationship and/or marriage?
>
> —Steve, age 37

> I think that a woman who is too independent may not want to follow the traditional gender roles in the context of marriage, and some men like myself would not like that.
>
> —Kevin, age 35

Being a strong, confident, motivated, and determined woman is a great thing. The problem comes when all of these traits start to distort and enter into conflict with God's original model for women. We were created to be fully dependent on God and should we choose to marry, to be able to submit to the love, protection, covering, and direction of another person.

> But I want you to understand that Christ is the *head* (authority over) of every man, and man is the *head* of woman, and God is the *head* of Christ. (1 Cor. 11:3, AMP)

The above scripture states that everybody, both men and women, must have a *head* (authority) over them. In the case of the single woman, the *head* that God has established over her are her parents or guardians. In the case of the married woman, her *head* is her husband (Eph. 5:23). It is advisable that those that are widowed or divorced seek the covering of a mature, spiritually minded person who can provide counsel, instruction, and accountability. This person may be their parents, another family member, a pastor, a church leader, or spiritual mentor. I will speak more about this subject of *authority* in the chapter called Honoring Your Parents.

God has established every authority. It is necessary that we learn to be teachable and moldable, and submit ourselves to the authorities that God has established over us so we can receive His blessings. The only exception to this principle is when our authority asks us to do something that goes against the will of God or that is sinful. In this case, we must obey God rather than men (Acts 5:29).

A godly independence

If you are a single woman, you should aspire to be able to take full responsibility of your own social and financial obligations while still living under the authority that God has established over you. In modern society, it is common to see that as soon as a woman starts working and earning her own money, she forgets to walk under authority. She leaves her home, sometimes at a very young age. There is no one who gives her advice, who shows her the right way; she has decided to direct her own life. She doesn't hold herself accountable to anyone to ask for direction, guidance, and even correction when needed. She might think, "If I can support myself, why should I submit to my parents? I am independent and grown-up." Unless she is truly seeking and following the direction of God wholeheartedly, she will likely have many struggles in life, exposing herself to many dangers. God did not design women to wander the world alone without having a covering of protection over them.

However, culture has had a big impact on how single people live. The idea of a single woman living with her parents until she gets married is, in many places, too conservative of a notion and becoming less common and accepted by society. In countries of North America and Europe, many single people leave their homes at a young age, sometimes before their twenties, to go to school or to look for a job. However, in other countries with more conservative cultures, such as in some of the Latin American and Asian countries, the idea of single women leaving their homes before they get married is seen as inappropriate, disrespectful to the family, and even as an act of rebellion. By comparing these two very different cultural scenarios, I want to highlight the fact that cultural patterns have a significant influence on people's lifestyles, choices, and decisions. So whether you chose to live with your parents until the day you get married or to leave your home before then, it's all about your culture, your values, and what you and your family consider to be good, appropriate, safe, and timely.

Whether you are a single woman who has lived with her parents all her life or you left your home at a young age, the important thing is that you never stop looking for the guidance of God and for the guidance of your parents. Even if you don't live with them, you can still ask for advice, receive correction, and follow their instruction. Your parents are the head that God has established over you until the day you marry. It requires a great deal of humility for a financially independent, strong, and mature person who can support herself to diligently seek the advice and direction of her authority and obey it.

Humility is putting your strength under the control of someone else. Jesus is the best example of a person with great power who was completely submitted to the will of His Father. He showed great humility when He did everything that His Father told Him to do and never acted by Himself.

Try to be a woman of meek and humble spirit, recognizing that you need God, because without Him, you are unable to do anything. Never forget that all you are, all you have, and all you have accomplished have been given to you by Him; so do not be prideful. Second, recognize that God has established a head (authority) over you. As you walk under this authority, there will be protection and blessing. It is important to resist the temptation of walking independently from God and your authority. The spirit of pride and independence won't take you anywhere; but humility and dependence on God will always lead you to make the right choices.

CHAPTER 7

THE THREE TEMPTATIONS YOU WILL FACE

Love rarely comes without temptation. The love that we see in many modern dating relationships is far from being the kind of love described in the Bible. According to 1 Corinthians 13:4–7, love does not dishonor others. It is not self-seeking. It does not delight in evil but rejoices with the truth. It is patient, it is kind, and it is not proud. However, many couples are having sex outside of marriage, which contradicts the definition of "love does not dishonor others." Also, it is common to see people having multiple love affairs, which contradicts the biblical principle of "love does not delight in evil." Furthermore, people are getting married for the wrong reasons, such as for the love of money, pressure from society, or pure physical and sexual attraction, which contradicts the biblical principle of "love is not self-seeking." All of these behaviors are rooted in temptation.

Temptation means "solicitation to that which is evil, and hence Satan is called 'the tempter' (Matt. 4:3)."[9] Jesus was tempted to disobey God. Satan still has this same goal in mind when he tempts us

---

[9] Easton, Matthew George. "Entry for Temptation." *Illustrated Bible Dictionary*, Third Edition, published by Thomas Nelson, 1897. *Bible Study Tools*, https://www.Biblestudytools.com/dictionary/temptation. Accessed January 17, 2018.

today. Disobedience to God is sin, and it separates us from Him. Satan uses temptation to deviate people from God's plans and purposes.

> Do not love the world or anything in the world. If anyone loves the world, love for the Father is not in them. For everything in the world—*the lust of the flesh, the lust of the eyes,* and *the pride of life*—comes not from the Father but from the world. The world and its desires pass away, but whoever does the will of God lives forever. (1 John 2:15–17, NIV)

According to the above scripture, there are three types of temptation that Satan will use to entice us to do evil: *the lust of the flesh, the lust of the eyes,* and *the pride of life.*

Lust means strong desire directed toward an object.[10] The *lust of the flesh* is what we do with our body to obtain ungodly gratification, satisfaction, or pleasure. The *lust of the eyes* is an ungodly desire to possess what we see or to have those things that have a visual appeal.[11] *The pride of life* is a temptation that aims at the self-exaltation of the individual. These three temptations are what the scripture calls the world and its desires, and loving them is contrary to loving God.

Satan used these three temptations to deceive Adam and Eve, and he was successful. Many years later, he used the same tactics to try to tempt Jesus; however, his efforts were to no avail. The same temptations that Satan used with Adam, Eve, and Jesus are the ones that he will be using with you. In the next section, I will explain each of these temptations in detail and will give perspectives on how they can affect your love life.

---

[10] Richards, Lawrence O. *New International Encyclopedia of Bible Words* (Grand Rapids, MI: Zondervan, 1991), p. 423.

[11] *Got Questions Ministries.* "What Is the Lust of the Eyes?" https://www.gotquestions.org/lust-of-the-eyes.html. Accessed March 28, 2018.

The lust of the flesh

Sexual immorality is a form of *the lust of the flesh*. However, *the lust of the flesh* is not always necessarily sexual; it also can be related to food, drinks, or substance abuse. Satan often seduces single people to have sexual intimacy outside of marriage. He knows your weaknesses perfectly, and he will look for opportunities to tempt you in those areas of vulnerability. He might introduce you to men that will awaken sexual passions and desires in you. Whether you want to feel loved and desired by a man sexually, or just enjoy the gratification and fun that sex can bring, you might be vulnerable to this temptation.

Sex is a good and beautiful thing. It is permissible and lawful as long as it takes place within the sacredness of marriage; that is the only place where God will bless it. Sex outside of marriage is sin (also called fornication and adultery); and it will only bring pain, condemnation, and suffering to those who practice it.

As you can see, even a good thing such as sex, if done outside the boundaries that God has established, is sin. Satan will constantly seduce you to cross and violate God's boundaries to commit sin, just as he seduced Eve in the Garden of Eden to eat from the one tree God had told her not to (Gen. 3:2–4).

Let me now share with you the story of Elena. She is a thirty-two-year-old single woman, still waiting for her prince charming. This is what she shared with me.

— 💕 —

I started having sex when I was twenty-four. It all started when the boyfriend I had began to put pressure on me saying that if we did not have sex, our relationship wouldn't work. I was not ready. I wanted to save my virginity for the man who would be my husband someday, which I thought would be him.

As I talked about this to my closest friends, who of course were not virgins, they gave me their opinions and advice on the matter.

"Elena, why do you want to save your virginity? You should be having fun. Once you do it the first time, the next time will not be difficult anymore," they said.

"Of course, I want to experience sex, but I feel it is wrong to do if I am not married," I responded.

"There's nothing wrong with it," they insisted. "It is the best way to get to know yourself and your partner. Sex is going to bring you both even closer. How are you going to know if you are sexually compatible? It is important that you know that before you decide to marry someone, don't you think?"

All these comments made me wonder if my conviction of waiting to have sex until marriage was something ridiculous, immature, old-fashioned, and childish. I began to see my virginity as something embarrassing and undesirable, and felt I had to get rid of it as soon as possible. For that reason, I agreed to have sex with my boyfriend. But as soon as we did, a horrible feeling of guilt and remorse began to torment me. Sex, although it gave me pleasure momentarily, was not a rewarding experience. Later on, my relationship with that guy, instead of getting stronger, gradually started to deteriorate and eventually ended. It had become merely a physical relationship, lacking in love, communication, and trust.

I am embarrassed to say that I had sex with another boyfriend and then with another. I have given away my heart and body several times only to be hurt, and left alone and empty. I don't want to continue in this path anymore. I want to wait and abstain from sex until marriage. However, I must confess that sexual temptation is something that I have found very difficult to resist ever since I did it that first time.

Do you see how Satan tempted Elena? He used her friends' advice to portray sex outside of marriage as something good, attractive, and fun. But in reality, all these things were a lie since sex outside of marriage will never be good. It is sin; and as such, it can destroy the mental, emotional, psychological, and physical health of people. Satan did not tell Elena the whole story; he just showed her the desirable side of it and threw her the hook. Elena found out about the undesirable side of the story later on, which included guilt, anguish, remorse, pain, and grief.

The lust of the eyes

The lust of the eyes will seduce you to desire things of this world more than God, thus turning the object of your lust into idolatry. Satan will use something outwardly attractive to generate an ungodly desire in you. If you are not careful enough to identify that what you desire is not from God, you might wrongfully pursue it.

When Satan tempted Eve to eat of the forbidden fruit, the Bible says that Eve saw that the fruit was *pleasing to the eye* (Gen. 3:6). Eve was seduced by the desirable appearance of the fruit, but the story would have been very different if Satan had tempted Eve with a rotten fruit full of worms. The devil will always present something that is outwardly very attractive to make us fall into temptation. As I already mentioned, he will only show us the desirable side of things and will then throw the hook. If we swallow it, we will soon discover the hidden, rotten side of the temptation.

How will Satan tempt you with *the lust of the eyes*? When you desire a man because of his physical attractiveness, fame, popularity, influence, wealth, or material possessions, then you are falling into this temptation. Satan can easily tempt you with someone who has these characteristics, diverting your attention from the traits that God wants you to be focused on.

A successful, single woman of advanced age once told me the following.

— ᥆᥎ —

"I just want to marry a man that is very handsome and that has lots of money," she said.

I immediately knew that she unknowingly was falling into the temptation of the lust of the eyes. Then I asked her, "If God brings you a man that looks different than what you expected and does not have a lot of money, but he is hardworking and can give you a modest life, and God says to you, 'I have chosen this man to be your husband,' what would you say?"

She got silent and thoughtful, and then she replied, "I think that God perfectly knows the desires of my heart, and He will fulfill them. There is nothing wrong in wanting to marry a man that I feel physically attracted to. There is also nothing wrong in wanting wealth and prosperity, right?"

———— ♡ ————

This woman was right in the fact that there is nothing wrong with desiring to marry someone attractive and with wealth. What is wrong is to want those things more than wanting God's will. She only paid attention to the first part of my question, which included the description of the man—what he looked like and had to offer—but she did not pay attention to what God said, "I have chosen this man to be your husband." She trusted more in what she thought was best for her instead of trusting God.

This woman's response denoted that she was not willing to accept God's plan regarding a partner unless it exactly matched the image she had imagined. Perhaps God often brought suitable men for her, and she was not able to recognize them because she was so focused on getting what she wanted. The truth is that all the encounters she had with men who were what she was looking for resulted in unsuccessful relationships.

> And even when you ask, you don't get it
> because your motives are all wrong—you want
> only what will give you pleasure. (James 4:3, NLT)

The problem with falling into the temptation of *the lust of eyes* is that we focus so much on obtaining what we want that we often overlook what is coming from the hand of God. Although many of God's blessings can have a wow factor and be astonishing and dazzling, there will also be times when the most beautiful blessings of God will simply come wrapped in newspaper. If we are not sensitive to His voice telling us, "This gift comes from Me," we may not be able to recognize it.

The pride of life

People who fall into the temptation of *the pride of life* are full of arrogance. They covet having power, control, fame, and popularity. They want to promote themselves to higher levels of recognition and influence.

Satan seduced Eve to eat from the forbidden tree, telling her that she would not die but that her eyes would be opened, and she *would be like God* (Gen. 3:5). Eve wanted to be like God and to have His power and wisdom; therefore, she ate the forbidden fruit and then offered it to her husband (Gen. 3: 6–7). Satan also tried to seduce Jesus to exalt himself and take advantage of his position as the Son of God. But Jesus was humble and remained in his position as a man instead of exalting Himself ahead of God's plan.

Many single women want to get married just to have the *married* status. Others want to have a relationship with the most handsome and popular man just to brag that they were the lucky ones that got him. Others want to marry the wealthy man because they love the idea of the material things that he can provide for them. All these cases are examples of *the pride of life*. In all these scenarios, the desire or motive to be in a relationship is wrong. Are you with him because you truly love him and cherish him? Or are you with him to get a false sense of security or status? Everything that awakens pride, arrogance, vanity, feelings of superiority, desires for popularity, and diverts your worship away from God will inevitably lead you to fall into this temptation.

This is Chelsea's story.

Chelsea had convinced herself to be in love with Ryan. In reality, she didn't love him; she loved the lifestyle, comfort, and (financial) security that he could provide for her. Although he was not a very good-looking guy and was a lot older than her, Ryan was a very wealthy man. He drove a shiny sports car and often took her to fancy restaurants, glamorous events, and parties. He traveled the world because of his successful international enterprise, and often invited Chelsea to come on business and pleasure trips with him. He had a nice apartment with all the commodities she could dream of.

Ryan went through two divorces in his life. He did not necessarily want to get married again, neither did he want more children than the four he already had with his previous wives. But he wanted to have a woman by his side. In exchange for comfort, security, and a glamorous life, Chelsea accepted being his lover. Deep within her, she knew she didn't love him, and she wasn't happy. She knew something was missing. The relationship lacked the spark, romance, and passion of a true love relationship, and the worst part was that she might never be able to fulfill her desire to be a mom. She sometimes regretted her decision, but that's the price she chose to pay for the pride of luxurious living.

— 💕 —

Sadly, Chelsea is an unhappy woman who was seduced by *the lust of the eyes* and *the pride of life*. Her desire for status, wealth, and recognition led her to make a detrimental decision. Several times, she thought about leaving Ryan and pursuing happiness with a man that truly loves her. She longs to love someone deeply and intimately, maybe even having children one day. But the fear of not finding that person and losing the security that she has with Ryan is a hard thing to let go of. Chelsea couldn't resist the same temptation that Satan presented to Jesus: "'All this I will give you,' he said, 'if you will bow down and worship me.'" (Matt. 4:8–9). Jesus chose what is right; he resisted *the pride of life* and instead chose to do the will of his Father. Chelsea chose wrong. She chose to love what the world has to offer instead of pursuing the will of God.

I encourage you to identify which temptations—*the lust of the flesh, the lust of the eyes,* or *the pride of life*—have had the greatest influence on the decisions you have made about choosing a partner. Once identified, surrender these areas of weakness to God, and ask Him for strength and wisdom to resist them. The best way to recognize the blessings of God and to separate them from the temptations Satan presents is to ask God to align our expectations to His will. Ask Him to give you discernment to recognize evil and wisdom to make the right choices.

CHAPTER 8

UNEQUALLY YOKED

Ellen is a Christian woman who faced the many challenges of being in a relationship with a man who did not believe in God. At first, their spiritual differences seemed to be small, manageable, and acceptable; but over time, they only created a huge division between the two. Poor communication, lack of understanding, intolerance, arguments, sadness, confusion, frustration, and sin are often the result of a relationship where God is not at the center. They were experiencing all of these problems and more. As the relationship deteriorated, Ellen realized there would be detrimental consequences if she married an unbeliever.

"I know God can transform his heart," Ellen said, "but what if that never happens?" Overwhelmed with questions without answers, she felt helpless and confused. She was in love with him, but things in their relationship were not going well at all. She was trapped in a great dilemma. Should she continue her relationship with this man despite the faith gap between them or should she let him go, trusting that God had a godly man in store for her?

This is their story.

A relationship without God

Ellen and Jim worked together at the same company. What started as a friendly work relationship rapidly turned into a romantic love affair. They got along very well and could have long conversations about many subjects they both enjoyed. Jim had many virtues that Ellen was looking for in a man. He was tall and handsome, and had a nice personality, strong family values, education, and success.

Jim began to eagerly pursue Ellen; he felt very attracted to her from the moment they met. Inevitably, the day came when Jim asked her to be his girlfriend, and Ellen excitingly accepted. She knew that Jim was not the kind of man that would waste her time. After all, they both were in their thirties, looking to settle down and find a person to spend the rest of their lives with.

However, there was an inconvenience. Ellen was Christian and Jim was not. Her long-time desire had been to marry a man of faith who loved God. Ellen knew that Jim was not the Christian man she had been praying for, but she thought that maybe she could lead him to Christ. There were so many things that she loved about him. For Ellen, Jim's lack of faith did not seem reason enough not to date him.

Jim did all the things that Ellen expected from him in order to please her. He started going to church with her and joined a Bible study. However, deep down, he was not interested in any of these things, and he felt uncomfortable with Ellen's faith. He wanted to find logical explanations to spiritual things and often debated about biblical subjects. He doubted the existence of God, and when the opportunity was presented to him, he refused to accept Jesus as his Savior.

They found themselves disagreeing on a lot of things, getting into arguments about faith and Christianity that made them upset and frustrated with each other. Ellen soon realized that the more she tried to share about her faith, the more they argued, and the problems only got worse. At first, she thought it was her job to convert Jim and make sure he received salvation; but later, she understood that only the Holy Spirit could do that.

Many times, they both felt disrespected, hurt, unloved, and unaccepted by the other. A lot of these problems were in fact a consequence of their spiritual differences. The relationship was growing distant, cold, and empty. Ellen felt so sad and unhappy. Jim simply did not understand Ellen's faith at all. It was like speaking different languages and living in separate worlds.

"Lord, why haven't You revealed Yourself to Jim? Why haven't you changed his heart?" Ellen prayed. God showed her that He was constantly trying to reveal Himself to Jim, but Jim had free will to decide which course to take. His decision so far had been not to give up his life to Christ, not to believe in God, not to repent and to continue living in sin. God showed Ellen that she had to let him go.

Ellen took courage and talked to Jim about her concerns because of their spiritual differences. She told him that their relationship was dysfunctional and couldn't continue. After arguing for a very long time, they were not able to fix anything. Finally, Jim said, "All this time, I did all those things that you wanted in order to make you happy. But my real intention was to get you out of church and put an end to that obsession you have about your God and Jesus. Apparently, God was always your priority. You always loved Him more than me!" These words were like a knife stabbed in Ellen's heart. In that moment, she realized that Jim had been lying to her all that time. Needless to say, they broke up that day.

— 💕 —

Love relationships between believers and nonbelievers are more difficult and dangerous than we think. They bring conflict, heartache, and frustration, and often fall into sin. The Bible says that there cannot be fellowship between light and darkness, believers and unbelievers (2 Cor. 6:14). This chapter will expand your perspective on what the Bible calls being *unequally yoked*.

What does it mean to be unequally yoked?

Do not be *yoked* together with unbelievers. For what do righteousness and wickedness have in common? Or what fellowship can light have with darkness? What harmony is there between Christ and Belial (Satan)? Or what does

a believer have in common with an unbeliever?
(2 Cor. 6:14–15, NIV)

Unequally yoked refers to the union of a believer in Christ with an unbeliever. In such union, both people will tend to pull in opposite directions; and the result will be disagreements, frustration, arguments, emotional pain, and ultimately, failure of the relationship.

A *yoke* is the wooden crosspiece that unites two animals, for example oxen or mules, to plow the soil. When animals are of the same strength, they are *equally yoked*; the load is evenly distributed between the two so they are able to move in a straight line and at the same pace. But when two animals of different strength are put together, for example an ox with a mule, they are *unequally yoked*; the result is that the strongest animal carries most of the load while the weakest one lags behind, causing the plow to veer off course. This makes the work more difficult, inefficient, and exhausting for both animals. The same thing happens in love relationships when a believer joins an unbeliever.

In an *unequally yoked* relationship, there can be no agreement or harmony. This is because a believer in Christ has received salvation and is spiritually alive, belonging to Christ. However, he who has not believed in Christ has not received salvation and is spiritually dead because of sin.

> As for you, you were *dead* in your transgressions and sins, in which you used to live when you followed the ways of this world... But because of his great love for us, God, who is rich in mercy, made us *alive with Christ* even when we were dead in transgressions—it is by grace you have been saved. (Eph. 2:1–2a, Eph. 2:4–5; NIV)

The union between a person that is *spiritually alive in Christ* with a person that is *spiritually dead in sin* often results in division because they operate in different realms. The believer is in the *realm of the Spirit,* and his or her desire is to please God and to turn away from sin. Whereas, the unbeliever is in the *realm of the flesh*, and his or her desire is to live according to the nature of sin. According to Romans 8:8–9, those who are in the *realm of the flesh* cannot please God. If you have received salvation through Christ, you are not in the *realm of the flesh* but are in the *realm of the Spirit*.

Understanding these differences between believers and unbelievers is so critical at the moment of choosing a partner. All kinds of love relationships represent a union between two people. If it is a courtship relationship, the union is emotional, mental, and physical to some extent. If it is a marriage relationship, the union is total—husband and wife become one flesh (Matt. 19:6). God's plan for marriage is that man and woman achieve total unity, walking in the same direction to seek Christ. However, when they are *unequally yoked*, their ideals about faith and life are very different, and there is no complete union and harmony.

Imagine that a believing wife wants her children to know God and be raised as Christians while her unbelieving husband is opposed to her taking them to church. Or imagine that a believing husband wants his unbelieving wife to be submissive and respect his authority as stated in Ephesians 5:22–24, but she instead rebels against his authority and does not respect him. What can a believing wife and an unbelieving husband have in common? Or what will lead them to obtain the total union in body, soul, and spirit that God designed for marriage? The answer is, sadly, nothing short of the unbeliever giving his or her life to Christ.

This does not mean that they cannot be compatible in many other areas such as sexually or intellectually. Even if they are unequally yoked, they can have a lot of common interests and be compatible in many other areas: business, sports, hobbies, art, music, travel, etc. However, the most important element that bonds a husband and wife together and keeps a marriage strong through ups and downs is this: faith in Christ. Without faith, there is no solid foundation to hold and sustain a relationship. Good sex will not save a marriage in times of crisis; neither will wealth nor compatibility in common interests. Some may say, "What about love? Love can save any marriage, right?" The answer is simple. To love in the fullest sense of the word, it is necessary to know God (1 John 4:7).

In his devotional for married couples called *One: A Marriage Devotional*, Jimmy Evans talks about God's special love, and how this is the only kind of love that can build the right foundation for marriage and other relationships. He wrote the following:

> There is an odd truth concerning love and marriage. Understanding it is an important key in making marriage and other relationships work. The truth is this: we don't have the ability to really love without the power of the Holy Spirit working through us. Our capacity to love is based on God giving us that ability, supernaturally, as we surrender to Him.
>
> So how are people able to "love" when they don't know God? They can't. At least they are not able to love with God's type of love. God's love is a special love the Bible calls agape. It is a love that flows out of the will and does not change. It is the most stable and predictable kind of love and the only type that can provide a lasting foundation in marriage.[12]

Jimmy Evans addresses the idea that *agape love*, the love that comes from God, is key for the success of love relationships. Without this kind of love, we basically cannot love other people in the love of Christ. Agape love is unconditional, sacrificial, honest, pure, constant, and everlasting; and it is a result of the Holy Spirit working through us. A marriage without agape love and knowledge of God will not be able to endure the trials and difficulties that life will present.

---

[12] Jimmy Evans and Marriage Today, *One: Marriage Devotional by Jimmy Evans*, Day 3. Accessed through *YouVersion Bible* on March 27, 2017.
https://www.Bible.com/en-GB/reading-plans/407-one-a-marriage-devotional/day/3

Three different ways of being unequally yoked

A lot of Christian singles have been deceived when dating people who do not know God or believers who are not committed to their faith. To make this concept of *unequally yoked* more understandable, let me explain three possible scenarios.

Scenario 1: When one person is a believer and the other isn't.

This scenario is the most obvious and easy to identify. The unbeliever does not want anything to do with faith, God, or the church. The unbeliever might say to his or her believing partner something like, "Look, you go to church and seek God if that is what makes you happy. I will respect your faith as long as you respect the fact that I am not interested in it." At first, it might seem quite convenient to give each other space and freedom to pursue different interests related to faith or the lack of it. However, in the long run, this scenario will end up causing division and the deterioration of the relationship. Ellen's story is a clear example of this scenario.

Scenario 2: A committed believer dating an uncommitted believer.

Christianity is a commitment to God. Christianity reflects *transformation* in the person who has given up his or her life to Christ. The fact that a person goes to church does not guarantee they are committed Christians. An uncommitted Christian continues to practice sin deliberately, does not pursue living a godly life, and lives in disobedience to God. Their lives do not reflect the fruits of the Holy Spirit, which are love, joy, peace, patience, kindness, goodness, faithfulness, gentleness, and self-control (Gal. 5:22–23).

Such people often deceive many genuine Christians who think they are dating another believer, when in reality, the person they are dating is far from being committed to Christ. Be aware that an uncommitted Christian may still be in the process of being transformed by God. However, it is unknown whether they will become a committed believer one day or will depart from God at any time. In this scenario, the risk is high because the believer-in-process can end up pulling a mature Christian away from God altogether.

— ❧ —

Vivian started dating Alexander who worked in ministry. She felt a deep admiration for him from the moment she met him. They began a romantic relationship almost immediately. As the relationship between them developed, Alexander confessed to her that he had a weakness for sex and women. In spite of his work and involvement in ministry, he had a long record of sexual partners, so much so that he had lost count. He acted like he had repented and walked away from that lifestyle, but Vivian did not know if he was sincere or if there was more to the story. For Vivian, this was a huge red flag, but she decided not to judge him and allow time for the truth to be shown.

Well, it didn't take that long for Vivian to receive a revelation about Alexander's heart. Whenever they went out, she perceived that Alexander could not take his eyes off other women; he looked at them with lust from head to toe. This made Vivian very uncomfortable. Alexander enjoyed going to casinos regularly; he also drank a lot of alcohol. She realized that he loved being the center of women's attention wherever he went. It was then that the Holy Spirit revealed to Vivian that although Alexander was a believer, he was not fully committed to Christ. She felt that continuing in a relationship with him was dangerous, so she ended the relationship soon after.

— ❧ —

Not every person who goes to church and calls himself or herself a Christian has committed their lives to God. It is necessary to ask the Holy Spirit for discernment to be able to identify when a person is truly committed to Christ or just pretending. There are many deceitful men and women out there who have an appearance of godliness, who pray and know the Bible, but whose hearts are far from God. They end up deceiving many genuine, committed believers.

Scenario 3: Believers of different denominations.

Christian believers of different denominations usually differ in many practices and ideas. Although they both believe in Christ, their interpretation of God's Word, salvation, and faith, as well as the way they conduct religious ceremonies and spiritual traditions, can be completely different from one denomination to another.

Imagine that you were raised in a Baptist church where ceremonies are normally performed in a very conservative manner; but your husband was raised in a Pentecostal church where speaking in tongues, clapping, jumping, dancing, and screaming is normal. Or imagine that you were raised in a Christian church where faith is placed only in God the Father, Christ, and the Holy Spirit; and your husband was raised in a Catholic church where faith is placed also in saints, the Virgin Mary, and various idols. These differences can cause some tension in your relationship; however, they can be manageable if you communicate well, respect each other's faith, and ultimately decide on one path to follow.

Each one of these scenarios has different complexities and cautions that you should consider carefully before moving forward into any of the above situations.

Are you dating an unbeliever?

Many believers date unbelievers thinking that they can convert them. However, *no one can convert anyone to Christ except the Holy Spirit.* Besides sharing the gospel and inviting an unbeliever to church, the most effective thing that you can do to help that person receive Christ is to pray for them.

It would be better for you not to pursue love relationships with an unbeliever until you know that he has given his life to Christ. If you are dating an unbeliever that has started to go to church with you, keep on praying for him and ask the Holy Spirit for discernment to be able to recognize if they are genuinely seeking God or just pretending.

If a person is an unbeliever, God can transform his life. For this transformation to happen, there should be true repentance and turning away from sin.

———— ♡ ————

A few years ago, a guy with drug problems named Robert arrived at the church I attended. Robert was hungry for God. God's love began to fill his life and gradually transformed him until he was free from all his addictions. Sometime later, Robert set his eyes on a girl who was also a member of the church. It turned out that she was the pastor's daughter. Robert was her secret admirer for a long time, and they developed a good friendship.

When he could not hide his feelings anymore, Robert took courage, approached the pastor, and confessed to him that he was in love with his daughter and that he believed that she was going to be his wife. The pastor looked at him and answered, "I am not so sure of that son. God has not told me anything about it." Robert felt discouraged for he knew that the pastor's daughter was far out of his league. He thought he didn't have a chance.

However, he remained faithful to God and kept going to church. He then began to serve God in various ministries of the church and became the leader of the men's group. No one imagined that this young leader had once arrived to church as a drug addict. Two years later, the pastor approached Robert. He placed his hand on his shoulder and said to him, "Son, your faithfulness to God has rewarded you. Now I know that you will be my daughter's husband."

———— ♡ ————

As with Robert, it is important that there is evidence and testimony that the person who was an unbeliever truly surrendered to Christ and is committed to God. The evidence is *transformation* in their life and character, *repentance* from their sins, and *turning away* from their old ways of living. You will be able to see it in his actions, for faith without actions is dead (James 2:17).

It will not be convenient in the long run

As a believer, you might be tempted to start a relationship with an unbeliever out of *convenience*. You might tell yourself that he has a great career, that he has so many other qualities you have been looking for, that nobody makes you feel the way he does, that you are extremely compatible in so many other things, that you are extremely attracted to him, and on and on and on. Many people think this way too. In their opinion, it is *convenient* to date someone that meets specific criteria even though that person does not believe in God. Believers often compromise their faith and begin relationships thinking that they can lead the other person to Christ. Some of these relationships will work, but many others will face great challenges because of obvious differences in their spirituality, morals, and values. Once love and feelings develop, it is very difficult to step out of these relationships without suffering great heartache. So why to take the risk?

There are success stories in which a believer marries an unbeliever and ends up leading him or her to Christ. I have heard testimonies in which after years of much prayer and spiritual warfare, the wife manages to lead her husband to Christ or vice versa. But these scenarios are exceptions and not the rule. They often come with a lot of heartache, distress, and pain. More often, they are stories of Christians who marry unbelievers and begin to falter in their faith. They stop praying, going to church, having fellowship with other believers, leading their children to God, etc., all because their spouses are unbelievers and do not want to participate in any of these activities, nor do they want their believing partner to participate in them. The risks of joining in unequally yoked relationships are very great.

> For how do you know, wife, whether you will save your husband [by leading him to Christ]? Or how do you know, husband, whether you will save your wife [by leading her to Christ]? (1 Cor. 7:16, AMP)

The answer to the above is: we do not know! The scriptures make it very clear that there is no guarantee that you will be able to lead your spouse to Christ if you end up marrying an unbeliever. Do not compromise your faith!

If you feel lonely because of being single, joining an unbeliever will only increase your loneliness as you see the difference in your hearts. It may even lead to a feeling of emptiness, constant feelings of being misunderstood, and perhaps even being attacked or rejected for your faith. The spiritual things you will want to talk about will be meaningless for them. The things you love about God, that you are passionate about, and that bring you the greatest fulfillment and joy, will not be understood by the unbelieving spouse. At the core of your relationship, there will not be much in common between you and that other person, unless of course the other person turns to God.

If you are in an unequally yoked relationship, I encourage you to pray and ask God for direction about what to do. Ask also for the advice of other Christian believers who love you. It may be your parents, your pastors, a Christian mentor, or a church leader. Seek God's direction and follow His lead. He might ask you to surrender that relationship to Him, and if that's the case, it is because He will bring someone else into your life. It is important that you and the person with whom you will unite for the rest of your life are walking in the same direction, seeking Christ.

If you already ended an unequally yoked relationship, maybe God allowed you to know that other person so that you could share your salvation story with him. God will send others to go and water the seed of truth that you sowed in that person's heart for He wants everyone to be saved. You can still continue to pray for that person. Other than that, there is nothing else for you to do. It is time for you to turn the page because you are about to start a new chapter in your life, hopefully, with a transformed believer this time!

CHAPTER 9

SEVEN ATTRIBUTES TO LOOK FOR IN A HUSBAND

When I was single, I wrote a letter to God describing the husband I wanted. The letter was very detailed on the physical and character attributes I was looking for. I prayed for this list continually, hoping that God would respond specifically to my requests. Now that I am a married woman, I have come to the conclusion that having a list of attributes can distract many believers from God's perfect plan. If your list is not made under the direction of the Holy Spirit, then you will mistakenly believe that what you desire is God's will for you, when in fact, it might not be. Every attribute on your list must be clearly endorsed by the Word of God.

I was one of those distracted women. I was so focused on finding the man described on my list that I was blinded to God's plan. When God introduced me to my husband, I almost let go of this blessing. I didn't know he was The One. He did not match the description that I had been praying for. Thankfully, God opened my eyes, and I was able to recognize him. The husband God gave me exceeded my expectations and the deepest longings of my heart. God knew exactly what I needed, better than I did.

Most people's standards for choosing a partner are physical attraction and chemistry rather than biblical attributes displayed by godly men and women. Usually, when people are physically attracted, they immediately think they are meant for each other. There is nothing wrong with being physically attracted to the person you want for your spouse; it is actually important. However, chemistry and physical attraction should not be the standard for choosing a partner. These two factors alone will never be enough to form lasting and successful love relationships.

God wants us to be *spiritually, emotionally,* and *physically* fulfilled in love. These three areas are always connected. The most important aspect of fulfillment in marriage is *spiritual,* which will lead to *emotional* fulfillment, and ultimately, *physical* fulfillment. If God is not the center of your marriage, how can you achieve complete emotional intimacy with your husband? And if you are not emotionally close to your husband, how can you achieve physical fulfillment? This is simply not possible.

In this chapter, I will focus on seven biblical attributes of a godly man that every woman should aspire to find when looking for a husband. These attributes will help you to attain *spiritual* fulfillment in your relationship, which in turn will also help you to be *emotionally* and *physically* fulfilled.

1. *A man who fears the Lord*

> And now, Israel, what does the Lord your God ask of you but to *fear the Lord* your God, to walk in *obedience to him,* to *love him,* to *serve the Lord* your God with all your heart and with all your soul. (Deut. 10:12, NIV)

"To fear God means to reject every competing deity and to serve Him only (Dt 6:13). Fear of the Lord is expressed by walking in all His ways, by loving Him, and by serving Him with all our heart and soul (Dt 10:12; Job 1:1; Ps 128:1)."[13] A man who fears the Lord is not the one who goes to church every Sunday, but the one

---

[13] Richards, Lawrence O. *New International Encyclopedia of Bible Words* (Grand Rapids, MI: Zondervan, 1991), pp. 272–273.

who seeks to please God in everything he does. He seeks to do what is righteous, honest, and moral not only in his relationships, but also in all matters of his life.

How can you recognize a man who fears the Lord? The most important indicator is that he will have a personal relationship with God. He will seek His direction, will walk in obedience to Him, and will try to honor Him in everything he does. Secondly, he will be clear and honest about his intentions toward you. He will strive to protect your heart and will not play with your feelings. Third, he will treat you with respect, physically, emotionally, and verbally. Finally, he will honor your parents.

If you want to find a man who fears the Lord, you need to be a woman who fears the Lord also. This is critical for the long-term success of any love relationship. If Christ is not the foundation upon which your relationship is built, it will be very weak, unable to stand firm in times of crisis or trouble. It will be like a house that was built on the ground without a foundation; when the floodwaters came, it collapsed (Luke 6:49). But a relationship centered in Christ is "like a man building a house, who dug down deep and laid the foundation on rock. When a flood came, the torrent struck that house but could not shake it, because it was well built," (Luke 6:48, NIV). The rock on which you must build your relationships, your marriage, and your entire life is Christ.

—— ♡♡ ——

Mary and Thomas are two believers who got married. They had two children. Unfortunately, they divorced seven years later. The reason for the divorce, they said, was "irreconcilable differences." Thomas never put God as his priority in the marriage. His priorities were his job, sports, and friends, among other things. Mary also had her own set of priorities and occupations. Because of that, neither of them prayed regularly, and they only went to church occasionally. Today, they acknowledge that they had been walking away from God for a long time.

Although they are both believers, they did not seek God to solve their marital problems. Although they call themselves Christians, they did not have the fear of the Lord. Most likely, if God had been at the center of their marriage and if they had cried out to Him in times of trouble, they would still be together. Those irreconcilable differences would have been overcome with God's help, bringing them closer and making their love stronger rather than separating them.

— 💞 —

It is not enough to find a man who goes to church on Sundays or calls himself a Christian. It is necessary to find a man who fears the Lord and who truly loves Him.

2. *A man of humble spirit*

> Don't be selfish; don't try to impress others. *Be humble*, thinking of others as better than yourselves. (Phil. 2:3, NLT)

Humility can be seen as a weakness, but nothing is further from the truth. There is power in humility. "True humility and fear of the Lord lead to riches, honor, and long life," (Prov. 22:4, NLT). A humble man submits to God's authority and obeys Him. He treats others with respect, is quick to ask for forgiveness and to forgive, and lives his life serving others.

"Humility in our relationship with God is seen when we refuse to stand in judgment on His Word but instead respond immediately, recognizing God as the ultimate authority in our life."[14] This means that a man who opposes or judges God's Word and refuses to submit to the lordship of Christ is a man lacking humility.

Lack of humility can sometimes lead to arrogance. The arrogant person boasts of his physical appearance, knowledge, skills, achieve-

---

[14] Richards, Lawrence O. *New International Encyclopedia of Bible Words* (Grand Rapids, MI: Zondervan, 1991), p. 347

ments, or possessions. He hardly recognizes his mistakes, finds it difficult to ask for forgiveness when he is wrong, and is easily offended.

Arrogance and pride go hand in hand, and they are the opposite of humility. A woman who marries a proud man will have a life of hardship. She will feel she is not enough for him. She will have to meet his high standards and expectations. She will be the one often asking for forgiveness when there is a problem because he rarely will. She will also need to praise him constantly for everything he does because he feeds his ego by feeling admired and praised by others.

The following is an example of a relationship with a man that didn't have humility.

— 💕 —

Nicole started dating a very good-looking guy. Because of his looks, many single women were attracted to him, and he knew it. He enjoyed having their attention, being praised for his looks, and admired for his accomplishments.

Nicole was flattered that he showed interest in her. However, she found that being the girlfriend of a man like him was not an easy task. She always needed to be stunning, flawless, and impeccable in her looks, clothing, and makeup. She soon realized that she needed to praise him for everything because she sensed that he found great gratification in that. "Oh, you are so handsome!" "You're the best!" "I'm so proud of you!" "Wow, I admire you so much!" were the things that Nicole often said to him.

When they had a problem, she frequently was the one seeking reconciliation because he didn't. Even if it had been his fault, he rarely admitted his mistakes. Nicole began to develop great insecurities since she never felt truly loved, cherished, or important to him. Obviously, such a superficial relationship did not go very far.

— 💕 —

Humility is important for the success of any relationship. When you look for a partner, look for a man who submits to God. Pay close attention to how he treats you. Is he nice and kind to you? Does he care about others or only about himself? Look for a man who is ready to ask for forgiveness and recognize his mistakes. You should never feel inferior to him or work too hard to meet his standards. The only standards you need to meet are God's.

3.   *A man of determination*

> Since Jacob was in love with Rachel, he told her father, "I'll work for you for seven years if you'll give me Rachel, your younger daughter, as my wife." (Gen. 29:18, NLT)

A man of determination knows what he wants and works hard for it until he gets it. In the realm of love, a determined man knows which woman he wants and will fight for her until he conquers her heart.

For a determined man, nothing is an obstacle great enough to stop him from fighting for the one he loves. He won't be stopped or discouraged by time, distance, finances, religion, culture, or family background. On the contrary, any obstacle will only make his interest and love for that woman grow even more. He has fixed his mind on the goal—to win the heart of the girl and make her his wife.

The Jacob of the Bible was a man with determination. From the moment he saw Rachel, he was captivated by her beauty and charm. It was truly love at first sight. Jacob so loved her that he worked for her father Laban seven years in exchange for Rachel's hand. The Bible says that his love for her was so strong that this time of waiting seemed to him but a few days (Gen. 29:20).

After having worked those seven years, Jacob was deceived by Laban. Instead of receiving Rachel as a wife, Laban gave him Leah, his oldest daughter. But the love and interest of Jacob for Rachel was so great that he agreed to work seven more years for her (Gen. 29:30).

Jacob is an example of a man with determination, willing to fight for the woman he loved. He worked fourteen years to marry her. How many women invert the roles and instead of allowing a man to fight for them, they fight for him? Sometimes, women think it is convenient to facilitate things for men by taking the first step. They are the ones who ask for his phone number, call him first, invite him to go out, pay the bill, move to the city or town where he lives, and the list goes on and on. Meanwhile, many of these men become passive and lose interest. Within every man's heart, there is a desire to be a warrior, to fight for the woman they love and conquer her heart. And within each woman's heart, there is a desire to be pursued and conquered by a man. A man will move heaven and earth in order to obtain the love of the woman he wants. If he doesn't, it is simply because he is not interested enough.

If you want to do yourself and the man who will be your husband a favor, do not pursue him. Do not facilitate things for him. Let him fight for you. Find out if he is a man with determination and whether or not he is willing to commit to you. Enjoy being pursued and courted. If he does not pursue you and fight for you, then forget about him, move on, and allow yourself to be found by a man like Jacob, a man with determination. You deserve it!

4. *A man ready for commitment*

It is better not to make a vow than to make
one and not fulfill it. (Eccles. 5:5, NIV)

A man of commitment does not make promises lightly, but when he does, he fulfills them. He will not allow a woman to invest her heart and feelings in him unless he wants to have a committed relationship with her. If he starts a relationship with a woman, it is because he sees potential to propose marriage to her at some point.

— ❧ —

It was very heartbreaking the day that Rodrigo told Erika he wasn't sure anymore about their relationship. Erika could not understand Rodrigo's sudden change. Rodrigo had told her several times during the year they were dating that he wanted to marry her. Now all of a sudden, Rodrigo was saying, "I need a break. I need time for myself."

"Rodrigo, why do you say that? Did I do something wrong?" Erika asked in shock.

"You're not the problem. It's me," he answered. "I do not know if I'm ready for commitment."

Erika was so heartbroken when she heard these words. "But why do you say you're not ready? We had talked about getting married many times. You were excited about it. What changed?" she insisted.

"I just need time and space," he said. "There are so many things that are happening in my life. My job is very demanding. There are projects that I would like to pursue."

"Rodrigo, you should have told me that from the beginning. I feel like you have been wasting my time. I had hopes and dreams about a future together. Are you saying that it is over?"

—— 💕 ——

Rodrigo is an example of a man who lacks commitment. These men may seem very committed to you, but as soon as they feel you are secure and highly emotionally invested, they become frightened and want to run away.

Rodrigo obviously did not weigh his words when he told Erika that he wanted to marry her someday. Erika took this as a love declaration and almost a marriage proposal; obviously, this was not the case. Thousands of women end up in relationships with men who are unwilling to commit or who are afraid to lose their freedom. These women spend valuable years of their lives waiting for a marriage proposal that never happens. Men that lack commitment feel comfortable in relationships without ties, without pressure, without responsibilities, while enjoying all the benefits.

Erika and Rodrigo fall into the classic example of *modern dating*, where the relationship starts out with so much hope and promise, but fades away because of a lack of commitment. Many dating relationships follow this same pattern; modern dating is such a broken model. A better model of dating is *courtship* because it has commitment tied to it.

Why do you waste your time and give your heart away to a man that is not committed to you? If you continue in this direction, you will end up having multiple relationships and heartbreaks. You will spend valuable years of your life in relationships that are not going to last.

It is possible that some men come and say to you, "God told me that you are going to be my wife." My advice is, do not believe it immediately! Men can act by impulse and say things based on emotions rather than conviction. There were a few men that said the same thing to me. Do you know how many of them I married? Only one. The one who really listened to God, who was patient enough to wait until I was ready, and who God also confirmed to my spirit as the one who was going to be my husband.

Spend time getting to know well the men that come into your life before you give your heart away. Build a good friendship first, especially with those that are interested in you romantically or are pursuing you. Do not rush into having a romantic physical relationship even if you really, really like them. Let me repeat again, *do not*. Guard your heart. Do not give it away until you meet a man of God who is really going to protect your heart and who is ready to commit to you. Do not play the modern dating game; instead, follow the godly model of *courtship*, which has proven successful for many couples.

5.   *A man of provision*

> Anyone who does not provide for their relatives, and especially for their own household, has denied the faith and is worse than an unbeliever. (1 Tim. 5:8, NIV)

A man of faith knows that the call to marriage is a call to provide for his wife and children. Provision is not only financial; but it also includes the physical, emotional, and spiritual dimensions. Let's see what each one of these dimensions consists of.

Financial provision. A man of financial provision is the one that supports his home by providing for food, clothing, and the vital needs of his wife and children. He is also financially responsible; he sets the right financial goals and spending priorities.

When you look for a man that can provide for you financially, you need to ask yourself the following questions: Does he have a stable job? Is his job decent? Is he responsible with his money? Is he a saver or a spender? Will he be able to provide for his own household one day?

Financial problems can cause a lot of distress in marriage. Interestingly, it's usually not the lack of finances that causes a divorce but rather it is spouses who have different spending priorities that end up having difficulties. According to the Austin Institute for the Study of Family and Culture, "24% of marriages in America would want a divorce because of having different financial priorities and spending patterns."[15] Imagine you are a saver, but the man you are dating is a spender. Or that either one of you has compromising spending habits such as overspending on shoes, clothing, drinking, going out to eat, or hobbies. Over time, these differences can cause tremendous tension in a relationship.

Before you marry someone, it is important to communicate well with your partner about financial goals, future expectations, and spending habits. Are you both willing and able to work? What kind of financial responsibilities are you going to be able to assume (i.e., buying a new home, a car, acquiring a business loan)? Do either of you have debts? If so, how are you going to handle those debts once you get married? Where are you going to live? Are you going to rent or buy a house, or are you going to move in with your parents?

---

[15] Austin Institute, "Divorce in America: Who Wants Out and Why," *The Austin Institute for the Study of Family and Culture,* April 9, 2014. http://www.austin-institute.org/research/divorce-in-america. Accessed March 17, 2017.

As a wife, if you are willing and able to come alongside your husband and work, that's fantastic! However, that should not relieve him from his responsibility as a provider of the household. When looking for a husband, try to find a man who is not only ready for commitment, but who also can be a financial provider.

Physical provision. A man of physical provision is the one that demonstrates affection through physical touch to the woman he loves. This affection can be in the form of hugs, kisses, and caresses.

A man who is not physically affectionate may be this way because he is not attracted or interested in the woman he is in a relationship with. He is too shy, he is too respectful of her, or he has other sexual preferences.

Whatever the scenario is, if you are in a relationship like that, you need to talk with your partner and share your concerns about the physical treatment or the lack of it. Physical interaction within the boundaries established during courtship is an important aspect in nurturing the love relationship.

Emotional provision. A man of emotional provision listens attentively to the woman he loves. He is interested in knowing what she feels, and he is willing to give advice and comfort. He demonstrates his love to her by speaking words of affirmation, comfort, and encouragement. A woman with a man like this knows he cares about her, that she is loved, cherished, and beautiful to him.

——— 💞 ———

Amy constantly complained about Jim's apathy. She usually did all the talking when they went out. Jim was a good listener, but he didn't talk much. They had been engaged for more than six months, and Amy did not know what was going on in Jim's head. She did not know his worries, dreams, or goals because he never talked about such things. Amy, on the other hand, talked about all these things, and more, concerning her life.

Amy often asked Jim, "How was your day today? How are you doing? What do you want to do later?" Jim's answers were always short and lacking in depth. "I am okay," or "I do not know," and sometimes, "Whatever you want to do," were common examples of his answers. Amy wanted to know Jim more deeply; but above all, she wanted a partner that talked to her heart, who nourished her emotions, and with whom she could have interesting and engaging conversations.

— 💕 —

Obviously, there was a big gap between Amy and Jim. Amy needed a man that had conversation. Jim, on the other hand, was the quiet type who did not talk much. Some women might have an affinity for and even enjoy men like that. But if that is not you and you need someone who speaks more and who nourishes you emotionally, then a man like Jim is not your match.

Spiritual provision. A man of spiritual provision loves and fears the Lord. He leads his household in faith. He provides godly counsel, wisdom, and correction to his family. This man understands the spiritual needs of his partner and responds to them, whether they are needs for prayer, fellowship, or godly advice. He is a man that strives toward leading the woman he loves to the knowledge of Christ, who prays for her, and knows that his most important role is to be head of his home.

If you want to marry a man who will be a spiritual provider for you and your future children, it is important that you pay close attention to what his relationship with God looks while you are dating him. Does he go to church? Does he pray? Is he a committed believer? Does he have a godly lifestyle? As already explained at the beginning of this chapter, it is very important to find a man who fears and loves the Lord.

6. *A man of leadership*

> *He must* manage his own household well,
> keeping his children under control with all dig-
> nity [keeping them respectful and well-behaved].
> (1 Tim. 3:4, AMP)

In modern society, many women are assuming the leadership role of the family. It is common to see this trend in marriages where men are passive and don't take their authority as the head of their household. However, this is contrary to what scripture teaches.

The Bible says, "The head of every man is Christ, and the head of the woman is man, and the head of Christ is God" (1 Cor. 11:3, NIV). This passage demonstrates a clear order of authority. The wife must submit to the authority of her husband, just as the husband must submit to the authority of Christ. Many abuse this verse by implying that women are inferior to men, but this is not the case. Although men and women are different and have been assigned different roles by God, these differences do not imply inferiority. What the Bible is saying is that "a woman ought to have authority over her own head" (1 Cor. 11:10, NIV).

A man of leadership assumes his role as the authority of his house. He leads his wife according to the Word of God, disciplines his children, and provides for the financial, physical, emotional, and spiritual needs of his family.

The ability to manage a household can be seen in a man while he is single. He is responsible and assumes his roles at work, home, church, and in society. He is a man with vision and goals, and knows where he is going. For a man to manage his household effectively, it is necessary that he be completely submitted to the authority of Christ.

7. *A man who loves you*

> Husbands, love your wives, just as Christ
> loved the church and gave himself up for her.
> (Eph. 5:25, NIV)

There are two kinds of love you can experience in a relationship. The first one is based on physical attraction and chemistry. It embraces sexual desire and is human in origin. This kind of love is called *eros*. The second kind of love is sacrificial and unconditional. It perseveres, is honest, and constant. Its origin is in God; it reflects His loving character. It is the kind of love displayed on the cross when Jesus died for all of us. This kind of love is called *agape*.

Most people seek love based on eros only. But eros alone will never be able to sustain a relationship or marriage. The combination of both, agape and eros love, should be experienced between husband and wife. However, since agape love comes from God, the only way a man can love you this way is if the love of Christ is in him.

> Love is patient, love is kind. It does not envy,
> it does not boast, it is not proud. It does not dis-
> honor others, it is not self-seeking, it is not easily
> angered, it keeps no record of wrongs. Love does
> not delight in evil but rejoices with the truth.
> It always protects, always trusts, always hopes,
> always perseveres. (1 Cor. 13:4–7, NIV)

The above scripture describes *agape* love. A man who loves you with agape love will persevere and will patiently wait for you until you are ready. He will respect you physically, emotionally, and verbally. He will accept you as you are. He will not try to change you, nor will he compare you with other women. He will not judge your faith. He will not be arrogant or proud. He will be able to forgive and ask for forgiveness. He will affirm his love for you with words. He will protect you. He won't give up easily; he will fight for you. And when you finally say *yes* to him, he will anxiously be looking forward to the day he takes you down that aisle.

I would like to encourage you to start praying for a man with the attributes found in the Word of God. I only described seven in this chapter, but as you read your Bible, you might find many more. The perfect man does not exist, yet the man God has for you will be exactly what you need, whether he has many or just a few of these attributes. Do not focus too much on his physical appearance or the material things he might have. These things, although not bad, will not be the ones that bring you true, everlasting happiness. My final advice is make God's Word your standard in finding your husband because in the end, that's the only guarantee for a successful love relationship.

CHAPTER 10

THE NAKED TRUTH ABOUT PREMARITAL SEX

> Flee from sexual immorality. All other sins
> a person commits are outside the body, but who-
> ever sins sexually, sins against their own body.
> (1 Cor. 6:18, NIV)

Consider the following:

Boy meets girl. She is everything that he has been looking for. She is beautiful, intelligent, and funny. She has a contagious smile and great confidence in herself. They start dating. Not only do they feel very physically attracted to each other, but they also have strong chemistry. After a couple of dates, they start kissing. Kisses become more passionate with time. Before long, they begin to feel sexual tension. They believe they are destined to be together and decide to consummate their love by having sex.

They find sex to be fun and exciting; they continue to have sex regularly. As the relationship evolves, they begin to realize they are not as compatible as they thought. They have very different lifestyles, interests, and priorities. These differences have caused arguments, verbal and emotional abuse, and deterioration of the relationship. They don't seem to understand each other anymore. Conflicts arise;

they grow cold and distant from each other. Inevitably, the relationship ends.

The differences they have are irreconcilable. They know it is best to follow separate paths and to continue looking for love somewhere else. But both have been deeply emotionally affected. She feels shattered and disappointed to have given away her virginity to a man she didn't end up marrying. He, on the other hand, has chosen to take an attitude of denial, hiding what he is truly feeling.

It's been two years since the breakup, and she still thinks about him. She is full of confusion, remorse, and guilt. She knows that the decision to break up was the best. Even still, she often asks herself why it did not work and if there was anything she could have done differently.

Others have pursued her, but she is hesitant to open her heart again. The breakup left a deep wound that has not healed. She holds resentment, fears, and insecurities. Without realizing it, she has been on guard, not letting anyone near her heart. Although she desires to fall in love again, she has not been able to start a new relationship.

He never accepted the pain of the breakup. Soon after, he started a relationship with another girl for the wrong motives. There was no love, only a desire to have sexual gratification and fill a great void.

Eventually, she healed and was able to move on. A couple of years later, she found love in the arms of another man. She got married, but soon, she discovered that those unpleasant memories and sexual thoughts from her past relationship kept resurfacing.

— ♡ —

Now let us think carefully. These people began the relationship with great expectations of a future together. They decided to make complete what they thought was love by having sex. In reality, what they felt was not love, but only feelings and emotions based on chemistry and physical attraction. Although they were sexually and physically compatible, they were not compatible intellectually, morally, and spiritually.

They thought that once they ended the relationship, it would just become a thing of the past. They thought they could successfully walk away from it without any repercussions in their future. That, unfortunately, was not what happened. Both were hurt for a long time after the breakup. Although they wanted to forget each other, they were not able to completely do so. Although they wanted to find love again, they were constantly barraged by fears, insecurities, and unpleasant memories; and they found it very difficult to trust people again.

For a long time, they were not able to find love or stay in love because they were wounded. They realized that their relationship had left them damaged, in effect, transforming them into different people. Sex not only united them physically, it also knit their souls together, creating a deep and hard-to-break, *ungodly emotional bond.*

Godly and ungodly emotional bonds

> For this reason a man will leave his father and mother and be united to his wife, and the two will become *one flesh.* (Eph. 5:31, NIV)

Most people think that it is okay to have premarital sex while using proper protection to avoid an unwanted pregnancy or a sexually transmitted disease. But there is more to sex than just a physical connection with physical consequences. Sex not only makes two people become one body (one flesh), it also knits their souls together, thus creating a powerful *emotional bond* between them.

Emotional bonds (commonly also referred to as *emotional ties* or *soul ties*) can be described as deep and powerful feelings and emotions formed by the relationship between two people. These emotional bonds affect the three dimensions of our soul: our mind (what we think), our will (what we decide), and our emotions (what we feel). People who are bonded might become dependent or attached to each other physically, emotionally, and mentally.

Emotional bonds can be godly or ungodly. If godly, the bond will be nourishing; it will produce affection, love, devotion, respect,

117

and loyalty. An example of a *godly emotional bond* is when husband and wife have sex as an act of love; this bond will continue to nourish their relationship in a good way.

If ungodly, the emotional bond will be detrimental, damaging, and toxic. It will produce fear, sadness, anguish, resentment, guilt, shame, jealousy, and other unwanted feelings. It can make a person miserable and unable to move on from their past. The deeper the bond, the more difficult it will be to break. An example of an *ungodly emotional bond* is when a person has been sexually abused and develops fears and insecurities that can last for the rest of their lives unless Jesus intervenes with healing.

Emotional bonds can be created with or without sex; however, sex just makes things more complex. It takes the bond to a whole new level. Premarital sex creates *ungodly emotional bonds* because the sexual act is rooted in sin. At first, the bond might not look negative at all; on the contrary, people might feel emotionally closer than ever before, just as it happened to the people in the story at the beginning of this chapter. However, sin takes its course; and sooner or later, there will be detrimental consequences.

Ungodly emotional bonds produce negative psychological and emotional dependence upon the person with whom the bond is formed. It is very common to hear stories of single women who had an exciting and fun relationship with their partner, but as soon as they had sex, the dynamics of their relationships changed. Here are descriptions of these changes in their own words:

- "I feel like now my partner is in complete control of our relationship. I feel so insecure."
- "I cannot see my relationship as objectively as before. My emotions have clouded the way I see things now."
- "I do not know when I became so needy of attention and affirmation. I wasn't like this at all."
- "I wish I knew what he thinks about me. Does he really love me?"
- "I wonder if he is losing interest."

Ungodly emotional bonds will constantly bring torment in the form of intrusive thoughts of guilt, remorse, fear, insecurity, sadness, and confusion.

Consequences of premarital sex

No matter how much you feel you are in love with your partner or how long you have been in a relationship with them, premarital sex is sin, and there are consequences that come with it. Premarital sex is not the result of two people *loving* each other but rather *lusting* after each other. God does not bless premarital sex; it opens a door for the devil to torment you and to act in your life.

The ungodly emotional bonds formed by premarital sex are like chains that keep two people captive in their souls. There are areas in their mind, will, and emotions that have been affected by sexual sin and that will need freedom and restoration. The feelings and emotions they might experience as a result of the ungodly emotional bonds they formed are often negative and destructive. For example, they might not be able to stop thinking about the other person long after the breakup, they might continue dwelling on the pain and hurt of the relationship, they might not be able to forgive the other person for real or imagined wrongs, they may have difficulty moving forward with their lives. If this ungodly bond is not broken, people can remain captive for a long time.

The problem is that when two people have premarital sex, they usually do not think their relationship can possibly come to an end. Neither do they think about the physical, emotional, and psychological dependence they are creating toward each other. Satan successfully convinces them of the common philosophies of, "If you love him, there is nothing wrong with having sex. Everyone does it. If you use protection, there will be no consequences. Enjoy the moment." They unknowingly are forming ungodly emotional bonds that are destructive.

Without the healing restoration of Jesus Christ, many people who have had multiple sexual partners in their lives may start feeling very confused about what they want, and may be unable to fall in love. If God does not heal their wounds, they will turn into shame, guilt, and confusion. Unhealed wounds can make it very difficult for people to find fulfillment in their future relationships and achieve sexual and emotional satisfaction in their marriage.

Some of the consequences of premarital sex include:

- feelings of guilt and remorse;
- not being able to move on from your past;
- difficulty opening your heart again and trusting others;
- emotional baggage taken into your new relationships;
- fears and insecurities; and
- shame.

Ungodly emotional bonds will affect the way you approach future relationships. You might become very guarded because you don't want to be hurt again. Sadly, a lot of believers are so wounded from past relationships that they are unable to recognize the man or woman that God is bringing to their lives. They might reject, ignore, and even mistreat that person and let go of the blessing.

Another major problem is the emotional baggage that people bring into their relationships. *Emotional baggage* refers to all the negative expectations that you bring to every new relationship that are a result of your previous negative experiences and relationships. Emotional baggage can present itself in the form of deep fears, insecurities, and negative emotions that have nothing to do with the new person you are starting a relationship with. Oftentimes, both people in a relationship are bringing emotional baggage from their past that will have an impact in their future. They don't feel free to open up, to be themselves, and to love freely.

Furthermore, premarital sex opens the door so that the devil can accuse you, attack you, and torment you, ultimately damaging and destroying the relationship you had with the other person. The devil cannot just come and do things to us because greater is God who lives in us than the devil who lives in this world (1 John 4:4). But when we are disobedient to God and participate in sin, we give *room, place,* and *opportunity* to Satan for acting in our lives (Eph. 4:7).

The most devastating consequence of premarital sex is that it separates you from God just as any other sin does. It deviates you from God's perfect plan. If you commit sexual immorality and do not stop and repent, and turn away from your sin, it will just lead you down a path toward more sin, separating you further from God.

God's plan for sex

God designed sex to be enjoyed exclusively within marriage. It was never God's plan that two unmarried people have sex, no matter how much they feel they love each other. He knows the deep emotional bond that sex creates between a man and a woman and how permanently wounded they would be if they separate.

Sex between a husband and a wife is a representation of the intimate union that God wants to have with us in spirit. Husband and wife become one flesh when they have sex, in the same manner that we become one with God in spirit when we receive salvation (Eph. 5:31, 1 Cor. 6:17).

Sex is sacred; it is God's wedding gift. He blesses sex when it is done within marriage. However, when two people have sex outside of marriage (this is also called *fornication*), they abuse this sacred gift, and it gets damaged and corrupted.

Take a moment to think about the beautiful white dress that you would like to wear on your wedding day. Now imagine that dress indelibly marked with the dark stain of every person you had sex with through the course of your life. The damage to the dress would be striking. If each stain represents your entanglement with a prospective husband, the entire dress represents the smudges and smears of the emotional devastation that you are likely carrying into your marriage, which was designed by God to be this fresh, pure, beautiful thing, unhindered by enemy complications.

Wow! No one wants to get married wearing a dress like that, right? But this is what happens when we engage in premarital sex. Fornication creates ungodly emotional bonds that cause much damage to the soul. The difference between the dress and the soul is that on the dress, the damage is clearly visible, whereas the damage to the soul cannot always be perceived by the eye.

But no matter what damage you have done, or others have done to your soul, fear not. Your heart, mind, and whole being are very valuable to God who can cleanse away the darkest stain. He can make you whole and clean again, just as that white dress was when it was brand new. He can heal the wounds and the pain caused by your previous relationships. He can set you free from the emotional baggage that you have been carrying so that you can trust and love again. There might still be consequences from your acts, but it is nothing that God can't help you overcome.

In premarital sex (or fornication), there is no covenant before God between people, as there is in marriage. So if the relationship does not work, it might seem convenient to end it and start a new relationship with another person. Unfortunately, the soul is fragile and delicate. When two people have sex, their souls are similar to two white sheets of paper glued together; it is impossible to separate them without causing damage and tearing them into pieces.

So they are no longer two, but one flesh.
Therefore what God has joined together, let no
one separate. (Matt.19:6, NIV)

God did not design or plan divorce for anyone. He knew the deep connection that would be created when two people have sex. If God does not want a husband and wife to divorce because of the deep and powerful union of body and soul, what makes us think that it is okay to have premarital sex and to separate when it is no longer convenient? What makes us think that there will be no consequences? Only a lack of wisdom can make us think that way.

If there is sin, there will be no blessing

When I was single, I once started a relationship with a Christian guy. From the beginning, I let him know about my commitment to

God not to have sex until marriage. Fortunately, he was in complete agreement with me.

To my surprise, he confessed to me the following: "You know, Cintia, in the past, I had sex with several of my girlfriends. I am not proud of that at all. I have repented and decided to renew my commitment to God of abstaining from sex until marriage. I was able to identify a very common pattern in each of those relationships where sex was in the mix. As soon as we added sex into the relationship, everything good that we had prior to that began to gradually deteriorate. I am convinced that premarital sex is going to ruin any further relationship I have. This time, I want to do things right."

His words were like music to my ears. I was so happy to have found someone who was in tune with my feeling about sex and my desire to please God. I thought that things would be easier for us, but Satan is very clever and skilled in deception and seduction.

In the beginning, everything was going very well between us. The relationship was fun and exciting. I felt that things were going the right way; I even thought he might be my husband. We stayed firm in our decision not to have sex. However, the relationship started to slowly turn more physical.

Suddenly, things began to change for the worse. Fears and doubts began to torment me. I didn't feel as confident as I was at first. I did not know if he was as emotionally invested in me as I was in him. I began to put my guard up, I had lost complete control over my emotions, and the relationship was no longer fun.

Conversations became increasingly meaningless, often interrupted by awkward silences. I felt that there was a huge gap between us. The initial excitement and spark had all vanished. I tried to revive all of that again and nothing worked. I cried as the relationship slowly died before my eyes with nothing I could do to rescue it. I cried out to God desperately. I asked Him to show me the root of the problem and why this was happening.

In the midst of my prayer, the Holy Spirit showed me the problem. He spoke to me and said, "My daughter, my presence cannot dwell with sin. This relationship will not prosper because my blessing is not in it."

I was shocked! "But, Lord, why do you say it is in sin? We haven't had sex," I said.

"It is not necessary to have sex for a relationship to be in sin," the Holy Spirit responded. "Your first sin was to forget about me, I am your first love. You made an idol of this relationship and turned away from me. Your second sin was that you did not keep your body, mind, and heart in holiness."

My heart sank when I had this revelation. He was right. I had made an idol of that relationship, and I had turned away from God. Then the Holy Spirit reminded me of the following scripture:

> But I tell you that anyone who looks at a woman *lustfully* has already committed adultery with her in his heart. (Matt. 5:28, NIV)

Lust is an ungodly desire toward an object or a person. It can produce a strong desire of wanting to have sex with someone that is not your spouse. This feeling is stimulated by sin. Inappropriate caresses and passionate kisses can easily open the door to lusting after someone sexually.

When the Holy Spirit reminded me of this scripture, I understood that my sin had not been the consummation of a physical act called intercourse, but a condition of my heart. I had been lusting after the guy I was dating, and he had been lusting after me too.

My heart was divided between a man and God, and the attitude of my heart regarding that relationship was wrong. These were sufficient reasons to grieve the Holy Spirit. God's presence was not in the midst of that relationship, and as a result, a whole wave of negative events started to unfold.

The relationship inevitably ended, and I suffered. I asked God forgiveness, I begged Him to help me overcome the pain of the breakup, and He did. With that, I learned an important lesson: sexual immorality doesn't start with the sexual act of intercourse; it starts in our heart and mind. Like most sins, sexual immorality starts with a seed of temptation in the form of a thought. If we entertain this thought long enough and do not stop it, it will bear its fruit— sin.

> Then, after desire has conceived, it gives birth to sin; and sin, when it is full-grown, gives birth to death. (James 1:15, NIV)

Our sin grieves the Holy Spirit. If there is sin in our relationships, God is not going to bless them.

Do not grieve the Holy Spirit

> And do not grieve the Holy Spirit of God, with whom you were sealed for the day of redemption. (Eph. 4:30, NIV)

When I made a promise to God that I would save my body for my husband, the biggest thing that stopped me from having sex was a desire not to grieve the Holy Spirit. The word *grieve* comes from the Greek word *lupeo,* which means, to affect with sadness, to cause grief, to make sorrowful and to offend.[16] Sin grieves the Holy Spirit.

The Holy Spirit is the third person of the Trinity (Father, Son, and Holy Spirit). He is God himself, yet He is usually the last one we think of when we approach God. He is the presence of God here on earth. When we receive salvation through faith in Jesus Christ, the Holy Spirit comes to dwell in our body and gives us power and self-control to resist temptation and to turn away from sin.

> Do you not know that *your bodies are temples of the Holy Spirit*, who is in you, whom you have received from God? You are not your own; you were bought at a price. Therefore honor God with your bodies. (1 Cor. 6:19–20, NIV)

---

[16] Thayer and Smith. "Greek Lexicon Entry for Lupeo." *The NAS New Testament Greek Lexicon,* 1999. *Bible Study Tools,* https://www.biblestudytools.com/lexicons/greek/nas/lupeo.html. Accessed March 29, 2018.

Once we receive salvation, our body becomes the temple of the Holy Spirit. But in order for him dwell in it, it is necessary that our body be a place worthy of his presence. When we deliberately participate in sexual immorality, the Holy Spirit convicts us of our sin. He lets us know that what we are doing is wrong. He always gives us the opportunity to repent and turn away from it. If we continue to do it and there is no repentance, we grieve him and we become blind, deaf, and spiritually dull to his presence.

When this happens, we will face various spiritual consequences:

- We lose the ability to hear God's voice.
- We feel lost and confused.
- We are tormented by various fears, guilt, and insecurities.
- We lose the power and strength that God gave us to do many things.

All because the Holy Spirit has been grieved.

We need to honor God with our bodies by not engaging in sexual immorality. The more we participate in sin, the farther we get from God.

It is never too late

If you have already had premarital sex, you might be thinking it is too late to repair the damage. However, it is never too late for God to redeem you, heal you, restore you, and deliver you from the bondage of sexual sin. He can do this for anyone who wants to turn away from sin and follow Christ.

Do not condemn yourself for past mistakes. Condemnation is a work of the enemy; he is always bringing affliction and torment in the form of intrusive thoughts such as, "I am not worthy of forgiveness. I am a bad person. I am dirty. I am guilty. God doesn't love me anymore."

In inspiring thoughts of condemnation, Satan's goal is that you believe that you do not deserve God's forgiveness and that He is angry with you. If you believe the enemy's lies, he will end up leading you further away from God, and you may continue falling deeper into sin.

Yet Jesus did not come to condemn the world because of sin, but to bring salvation and redemption to all who believe in Him (John 3:17–18.) If you think your sin is too bad for God to forgive, observe what Jesus said:

> Jesus answered them, "It is not the healthy who need a doctor, but the sick. I have not come to call the righteous, but sinners to *repentance*."
> (Luke 5:31–32, NIV)

Jesus came precisely for those who needed forgiveness and salvation. He came for all sinners; He came for you and for me. But notice that there is an important requirement to obtain forgiveness and salvation; the requirement is true repentance. Many people confuse repentance with remorse. *Remorse* is feeling guilt for doing wrong; however, remorse does not imply a change of attitude or direction. *Repentance* is being sorry enough about your sins to stop. It involves turning from a previous way.[17] Repentance implies a change of direction—turning away from evil and following God's way.

For many, turning away from sexual sin might seem difficult or impossible. But nothing is impossible with God; He gives us power and self-control over sin. Instead of sin dominating us, the Holy Spirit that dwells in us helps us to overcome temptation, and He delivers us from the bondage of sin.

> I have been crucified with Christ and I no longer live, but Christ lives in me. The life I now live in the body, I live by faith in the Son of God, who loved me and gave himself for me.
> (Gal. 2:20, NIV)

---

[17] Richards, Lawrence O. *New International Encyclopedia of Bible Words* (Grand Rapids, MI: Zondervan, 1991), p. 522

When we give our life to Christ, there is a change of nature within us. We are no longer those who were once dominated by sin and inclined to do evil. We are controlled not by the flesh, but by the Spirit, because the Spirit of God lives in us (Rom. 8:9). If the Spirit of God lives in us, He gives us power to resist temptation, and He puts in us a desire to do what is right.

If you want to repent and ask God to set you free from sexual sin and from the emotional bonds that were created because of it, you can say a prayer like the following or use your own words:

> Lord, I confess I have sinned against You and against my own body. I repent and ask for your forgiveness.
>
> Holy Spirit, break right now any ungodly emotional bonds that were formed with the person(s) that I had sex with in the past. Set me free from the consequences of these bonds such fear, guilt, shame, and insecurity. Heal my wounds and make me a woman that is whole, restored in body, spirit, and soul.
>
> Lord, give me power and self-control to resist sexual temptation. Teach me how to flee from it when it presents itself. From now on, I decide to keep my body and heart in purity, to abstain from sex and wait patiently until marriage. In the name of Jesus. Amen.

Let the Holy Spirit speak to your heart for a moment. Stay silent, close your eyes, and set your mind on God. Maybe He will show you what changes you have to make from now on to redirect your life on the right path.

It is possible that you will have to face important and difficult decisions such as ending a love relationship that is in sin or having a serious conversation with your boyfriend about your new commitment to God. As difficult as any of these decisions may seem, God will help you to walk in the right direction, and He will provide everything you need so that you can keep your commitment to purity. It's a matter of making a decision of faith and following the lead of the Holy Spirit.

Are you willing to pay the price?

We all want the blessing of God in our lives and relationships, but we must be willing to pay a price for that. The price is having a body, heart, and soul completely consecrated to Christ. It is good to desire living in holiness and purity, but desire alone is not enough; it is necessary to do everything we can to reach that goal. Giving up our lives to Christ requires a commitment on our part to turn away from worldliness and sin, and to be obedient to God.

> Then Jesus said to his disciples, "Whoever wants to be my disciple must *deny themselves* and *take up their cross* and *follow me.* For whoever wants to save their life will lose it, but whoever loses their life for me will find it." (Matt. 16:24–25, NIV)

Becoming Christ's followers is hard because we must constantly deny ourselves. *Denying ourselves* means giving up our natural desires and impulses in order to walk in the same way that Christ did, led by the Holy Spirit. No longer should we pursue what we want, but what God wants. No longer should we be seduced and dominated by sin, but we should aim to live in holiness, set apart for God and His purposes.

Fear should not be what stops you from having premarital sex, whether it is fear of getting pregnant, fear of getting infected by a sexually transmitted disease, or fear of developing an ungodly emotional bond. What must stop us from engaging in sexual immorality or any other kind of sin is our love, gratitude, and faithfulness to God. God's love is the greatest power in the universe, which gives us self-control not to fall into temptation. Our love for God will make us disgusted by sin and will set in our hearts a desire for *holiness*, the most sublime and excellent goal to pursue.

CHAPTER 11

MOVING ON FROM YOUR PAST

If you have ever had a breakup, you most likely went through the painful process of playing over in your mind memories from the past with that person. Maybe you imagined that relationship would be a "happily ever after," and it wasn't. You might now be tormented by intrusive thoughts and questions such as, "What did I do wrong? Was there anything I could have done differently? Am I good enough? What can I do to get him back?" Dwelling on the past only brings grief and sadness; it kills our joy. It is similar to being captive in prison; it keeps us from receiving what the future holds for us. One of Satan's goals is for you to dwell on your past, looking back instead of looking forward. He wants to destroy your faith and hope, convincing you that there will be nothing better in your future. God, on the contrary, wants you to let go of your past and keep walking forward, believing that the best is yet to come.

Everything that happens to us in this life is either God-*allowed* or God-*arranged*. What the enemy meant to use for our destruction, God will use for our good. He takes our ashes when we offer them to Him, and forms them into something beautiful, even with the painful experiences that we go through. The signature move of God is that He uses even the dead things in us for purposes of life.

> And we know that *in all things* God works
> for *the good* of those who love him, who have been
> called according to his purpose. (Rom. 8:28, NIV)

What this scripture is saying is that *in all things*, whether good or bad, God works for our *good*. Whatever happens to us, God will use it for our good to fulfill His glorious purpose in us. But pay close attention. This promise is not for everyone, but only for *those who love Him*. If you love God, if you seek Him and commit your ways to Him, then He will use every situation that you go through to shape you, strengthen you, and prepare you for the good plans and purposes He has in store for you, whether these plans are for your temporal good or for your eternal good.

If a relationship you started did not work, perhaps it was because that was not God's will for your life. For a time, He may have allowed you to be in that relationship to accomplish something in you and in the other person. Maybe God used that relationship to shape your character and faith. Maybe He will use the ashes of that relationship to bring beauty and healing to someone else's life.

I am convinced that God *allows* many singles to start relationships with people that they were never meant to be with in the first place. These relationships might result in hurt and pain. We need to understand that God gives us free will to make our own decisions even though they may not always be right. God allows us to commit mistakes so that we can grow from them and discover who we are, equipping us to make better decisions in the future. This falls under the definition of God's permissive will. The *permissive will* of God is what God allows even if it is sin and violates His *perfect will*. However, the permissive will of God leads to the accomplishment of His plans.

I thank God for the relationships that He allowed me to have before I met my husband. Although I was disappointed and hurt many times, I learned from my mistakes. My heart and character were shaped, my faith was strengthened, and somehow, all of those relationships prepared me to receive the blessing of my husband.

God does not want us to be stuck in the past though, dwelling on our failed relationships. He wants us to turn the page, move on, and conquer the promises and blessings that are ahead of us.

> Forget the former things; *do not dwell on the past*. See, I am doing a new thing! Now it springs up; do you not perceive it? I am making a way in the wilderness and streams in the wasteland. (Isa. 43:18–19, NIV)

God promises that as we move on from our past, new and good things will come. He is always doing something new for us; He is always working on our behalf. Even though we may not see what He is doing, it is already happening! God is lining up a series of impossible and supernatural events so that in His appointed time, you will meet the man who will be your husband.

Seven years before I met my husband, God blessed me with a job that I could do from home. I was working for a foreign company for which I wrote exhaustive and tedious business reports. It was very comfortable to work in my pajamas, not having to face the horrible city traffic. However, that job was very isolating; I didn't really have face-to-face interaction with anybody except my family. I spent countless silent hours working at a desk, staring at a computer. Many times, I thought that it would be very difficult to meet somebody, spending all of my days locked up at home, working. Sometimes, I joked that maybe God would bring my husband to my door one day. But deep down, I felt sadness because I knew that would never happen.

After seven years of working in this isolating environment, God finally took me out of my house and sent me on a long trip that lasted several months. The only thing that allowed me to do this trip was precisely the job I had. Although my geographical location was different, I still could work remotely, making money to pay all my travel expenses.

During that trip, I met my husband. Before I even started that job, God knew that I would need it to meet my husband one day. By giving me that job, God was opening a way to fulfill my destiny. I had no idea that I was already walking the road to my destiny while I was isolated, working from home.

Not only did God bless me with a husband, He also gave me a calling. He said to me, "Cintia, you will no longer be a business writer. I have called you to be a Christian writer. You will write for Me. The job I gave to you was only your preparation and training for this purpose. With all you have learned, you are now ready to fulfill your calling."

I never imagined that those seven years of isolation were, in fact, the road I had to walk to receive my love's promise, my calling, and to fulfill God's purpose.

The reason I am sharing this story with you is because maybe, you are right where I was, in a stage of life where you do not see how or when the blessing you are waiting for will come. Maybe you have wondered how God will make it happen. Perhaps everything around you is always the same, and nothing is changing. My advice is take heart! It is possible that without knowing it, you are exactly where God wants you to be, walking the path that He has prepared to bless you. Be in tune with the Holy Spirit; pray and ask for direction. If you need to make any changes in your routine or lifestyle, God is going to show you what to do.

Forget what lies behind and reach forward to what lies ahead

> Brothers and sisters, I do not consider that
> I have made it my own yet; but one thing I do:
> *forgetting what lies behind and reaching forward to*
> *what lies ahead*, I press on toward the goal to win
> the [heavenly] prize of the upward call of God in
> Christ Jesus. (Phil. 3:13–14, AMP)

The apostle Paul could not have said it better. What is your goal? Do you want to find a husband and have a Christ-centered marriage? Then you have to forget what lies behind and reach forward to what lies ahead.

Read each of the following questions and answer them honestly:

- Has it been more than a year since you ended a relationship? Are you still thinking about it? Or about him?
- Are you holding fears and insecurities because of what someone did to you in the past?
- Do you fear being hurt again?
- Do you think you might not be able to find love because all your past relationships have failed?
- Do you feel it's going to be difficult for you to trust a man again?

If you responded *yes* to any of the above then, *you have not forgotten what lies behind.*

- Are you depressed and isolated because of your breakup?
- Are you considering going back to a relationship that has already ended?
- Are you living in monotony: same routine, same friends, same activities, and same hobbies for years?
- Has it been a long time since you tried something new and stepped out of your comfort zone?

If you responded *yes* to any of the above then, *you have not reached forward to what lies ahead.*

The unknown is sometimes uncomfortable because we want to know everything and have control of all things. But this is not always going to be possible because only God has control of all things and only He knows the future. The things that God is preparing for your future are yet to be known and revealed; in the meantime, they are a mystery. But we do know those things will always be for our good; therefore, we should not be afraid of what is to come. We must forget and let go of the former things in order to be ready to receive the new things that God has in store for us.

Do you remember the story I shared in the first chapter about my relationship with the guy I met in Canada? I had really cherished that relationship. I felt that person was the best thing that had happened to me. However, God asked me to surrender that relationship to Him. The Holy Spirit brought a conviction to my heart that this relationship was not God's plan for my life.

I was obedient to God's instruction, and I let him go. However, for about two years, I dwelt in the past, replaying memories, remembering moments and conversations I had with that guy. I was not living my present. I was living in my past and longing to go back to it. I often wondered if I had made the right decision about ending that relationship. I even questioned if I had correctly heard the voice of God. Sometimes I thought that maybe God would bring us back together again. I wanted to save that relationship, but the Holy Spirit reminded me over and over again that God had a different plan.

One day, God spoke to me in prayer and said, "My daughter, stop turning to your right or to your left. Do not look back but look straight ahead. Set your eyes on Me. I have the future that you hope for. Keep walking forward and trust Me. If you keep looking back, one day you'll realize all the time you wasted dwelling on your past."

God knew my thoughts and my struggles as I continued looking back, longing for that past love. When God spoke to me, He gave three instructions:

- *"Stop turning to your right or to your left,"* which means, don't get distracted. Don't let your mind to wander; don't lose focus on what is ahead.
- *"Do not look back."* Looking back represents living in the past, without hope, walking without faith. It is essentially believing that the best has already happened and that the future holds nothing better.
- *"Keep walking forward and trust Me,"* which means, walk with faith, believing what God has promised and that the best things are yet to come.

These are things that God spoke to my heart, but I truly believe that these are instructions that every single believer should strive to follow.

If you think that you are supposed to get back together with someone you broke up with, let God confirm it. You do not have to do anything to make that happen other than praying. God does not need your help; on the contrary, your attempts to help Him could be counterproductive and could delay God's purpose for you.

The man who really is interested in you and who is destined to be your husband will do everything possible to get you back. You do not have to text him, call him, or send smoke signals or love letters. Neither do you need to prepare seemingly accidental encounters that you planned. Let him think of you, miss you, meditate on the mistakes he made, and let him find ways to get you back if that is what he wants.

Let him fight for you and have the satisfaction of pursuing you and winning you back. If after a few months of the breakup he doesn't do any of this, it is a clear sign that this man was not meant to be with you. Maybe he is not willing to fight for you or maybe he has already turned the page. If that's the case, the best thing you can do for yourself is to let him go.

Longing for something better

Cindy had a relationship with John. After six months of dating, John didn't seem as interested in her as he was in the beginning. John's calls became less and less frequent. When he picked her up to go somewhere, he didn't show any excitement or enthusiasm about being with her. When they were together, there were many moments of awkward and uncomfortable silence.

Cindy loved John, and she felt sad about getting John's cold treatment. When she shared with him the way she felt, he comforted her by saying, "I am sorry you feel that way. Everything is all right between us—nothing is wrong. I've just been a little bit stressed at work, that's it." Cindy accepted this excuse for a while, but over time, things did not change; they just kept getting worse. She knew this was not a healthy relationship, and she wasn't sure anymore if it was worth continuing.

Cindy prayed about it and felt a conviction that God had something better in store for her. She had dignity and knew her worth.

She knew she deserved a man who was deeply and madly in love with her, ready to fight for her heart. That was exactly what she told John. She said, "John, I've been praying about our relationship, and this is not the kind of relationship I've been praying or waiting for. I have been trying so hard for this to work, and all I am getting back is you becoming more distant, disinterested, and cold. I feel unloved. I think it is best to end our relationship."

At first, John looked puzzled. He could not believe what he was hearing from Cindy. But John did not try to fix anything, he just responded, "Well, this is who I am. I gave my best. Sorry if I could not meet your expectations."

That was not the answer that Cindy was expecting from him. She hoped John would try a bit harder and save the relationship, but that was not the case. He didn't fight at all.

Obviously, it took Cindy time to get over John and get healed. Deep down, she was hoping that John would miss her and come back, but he didn't even text her again. Sometimes, Cindy felt the urge to contact him but refrained. She knew she could not settle for less than what she knew God had promised her, a man that would cherish her heart.

— 💕 —

Cindy could have returned to her relationship with John if she wanted to, but she no longer wanted a mediocre and empty relationship. She aspired to something better, a relationship that came from God, full of excitement, romance, and commitment. When God saw Cindy's faith, He rewarded her in His time with a godly and loving husband.

> If they had been thinking of the country they had left, they would have had opportunity to return. Instead, they were longing for a better country—a heavenly one. Therefore God is not ashamed to be called their God, for he has prepared a city for them. (Heb. 11:15–16, NIV)

Read the previous scripture again, replacing the word *country* with the word *relationship,* and the word *city* with the words *godly husband.* Do you understand the message? The reason why you are not coming back to the mediocre relationships you have left is because you are longing for God's best, for what He has prepared for you, a relationship with a godly man that loves you, cherishes you, and commits to you.

When you forget what lies behind and reach forward to what God has promised you, God does not hesitate to reward your faith and give you His blessing. God's blessings do not compare at all to what you let go; they far exceed anything you have imagined.

Why it is not good to dwell on your past

There are several important reasons why it is not good to continue dwelling on your past relationships. Let me mention a few:

- *It can become an obstacle for you to open up to love again.* When your mind and heart are dwelling in a past relationship, it is very difficult to move forward and explore relationships with other people. Do not waste your precious time and emotions on something that is not worth it. Remember, a man who loves you is going to fight to get you back. But whether that happens or not, open yourself to the opportunity of meeting new people. Enjoy your singleness, make new friends, and explore new avenues of love when they present themselves to you. Maybe at first it is going to be difficult because you are still thinking about the other person, but that's going to change over time.

- *It will create fears and insecurities.* The most detrimental thing about dwelling in the past is to think that the same painful experiences and disappointments will repeat themselves over again. Do not allow these fears to take control of you! Move forward confidently. The blessings of God do not add sorrow with them (Prov. 10:22). If the blessing of

God is what you are waiting for, then you have nothing to fear.

- *You will start making destructive comparisons.* Some people make comparisons of their current relationship with their past relationships. They compare both good and bad things. For example, if your previous boyfriend sent you flowers every week and the one you currently have only sends you flowers on special occasions, you might think your current boyfriend does not love you as much. Or maybe your previous boyfriend was unfaithful and now you panic if your current boyfriend does not answer the phone because you think he might be with another person.

  Making comparisons can be offensive and unfair to the person you are dating and can be very destructive. My advice is to not let any past relationship become your standard of comparison. Let your standard of comparison be God's Word and what He has spoken to your heart. The past is in the past, and you should not compare it with your present or with your future.

- *The healing process will take much longer.* Healing the wounds of a breakup can take a couple of weeks, months, years, or a lifetime. The amount of time depends on your attitude and determination to move on. It is a decision that you need to make—whether to hold on to your past or forget about it and keep moving forward. Life is too short to get stuck in the negatives.

Do not distort reality

Sometimes, Cindy felt guilty about ending her relationship with John. She feared that John indeed had a lot of pressure from work and she hadn't been understanding of that. She kept thinking about him and missing him. She only remembered the good times but rarely thought about the reasons why she had decided to end the relationship: lack of interest, cold and distant treatment, poor communication. Cindy's parents helped her see objectively what her emotions didn't let her. This kept her from going back. What she was missing was simply a distortion of reality, something that had never existed.

For some strange reason, when a relationship ends, people tend to remember just the good times, often forgetting the things that led them to break up. Feelings and emotions sometimes cloud our mind, distorting reality. We then see things in what I call *the fog of fantasy.* For example, we think of the moments when the other person told us, "I love you," the fun dates, the first kiss, or that love letter received on Valentine's Day.

Yes, all those might be good memories, but were you really happy? Did the good moments outweigh the bad moments? When you feel sad thinking about the good times that you once had, do not rush immediately to text or call the other person. Rather, talk first to someone who loves you, like your parents or siblings, your pastor, or a best friend. They will help you see reality in an objective way. They will be your support when you feel overwhelmed by emotions, and they will not allow you to go back to a relationship that was not good for you in the first place.

I want to encourage you to turn the page and move on from your past relationships. Set your eyes on God and move forward. The day will come when you see your past relationships as an instrument that God used to fulfill his delicate and wise purpose in you. You may even feel grateful to the people you dated in spite of the pain that they may have caused you. Thanks to all of them, you matured, learned from your mistakes, and realized what you wanted. Most likely, your character was shaped and your faith was strengthened. Maybe it was necessary for you to go through those painful disappointments to get to the place where you are now. Keep your head up and do not lose heart. The best is yet to come!

CHAPTER 12

HEARING FROM GOD, TAKING ACTION

Everything you have read so far in this book has focused on the importance of *waiting* for God to bring love into your life. Does waiting mean staying still indefinitely in expectation of something eventually happening? To what extent does God call us to leave our comfort zone and walk in faith? This chapter will perhaps change your perspective about waiting. While God often calls us to wait for a season without any action on our part, undoubtedly the time will come when He also will call us to *take action* to accomplish His purposes.

Many people have been single for years due largely to the fact that in those years, nothing has changed in their lives. For many of them, everything is exactly the same as it was one, three, five, ten, or more years ago. They still hang out with the same circle of friends, pursue the same hobbies, and carry out the same routine every day.

Perhaps these people have grown comfortable following the same routine. Perhaps staying in the same place, with the same people, doing exactly the same things day in and day out gives them a sense of safety. However, this kind of monotony and lack of personal growth can eventually cause sadness and discouragement because God did not create us to have monotonous lives.

In your pursuit of love, it is going to be extremely important to have the guidance of the Holy Spirit to attain success in this area. In this chapter, I will talk about when God calls us to take an *action of faith* to leave our comfort zone. First, we need to understand what an action of faith is. Then, we need to understand how to discern when God is calling us to act in faith and leave behind what is familiar in order to receive *the blessing*.

What is an action of faith?

Almost all the characters in the Bible who achieved great feats, conquered kingdoms, won victories, and received God's promises, first had to put their faith into action.

Faith comes by hearing, and hearing by the Word of God (Rom. 10:17). This means that our faith is demonstrated when we first *hear* what God has said and then we *walk* in it. *For an action to be of faith, it has to meet an important requirement: it must be initiated, inspired, and directed by God and not by human will.*

Let's see a few biblical examples of people who heard God's instruction and then put their faith into action.

Noah

God's instruction:

> So make yourself an ark of cypress wood; make rooms in it and coat it with pitch inside and out . . . I am going to bring floodwaters on the earth to destroy all life under the heavens, every creature that has the breath of life in it. Everything on earth will perish. (Gen. 6:14, 17; NIV)

Action of faith:

> *It was by faith* that Noah built a large boat to save his family from the flood. *He obeyed God,*

who warned him about things that had never happened before. (Heb. 11: 7, NLT)

Abraham

God's instruction:

> The Lord had said to Abram, "Leave your native country, your relatives, and your father's family, and go to the land that I will show you." (Gen. 12:1, NLT)

Action of faith:

> *It was by faith* that *Abraham obeyed when God* called him to leave home and go to another land that God would give him as his inheritance. He went without knowing where he was going. (Heb. 11: 8, NLT)

Moses

God's instruction:

> Look! The cry of the people of Israel has reached me, and I have seen how harshly the Egyptians abuse them. Now go, for I am sending you to Pharaoh. You must lead my people of Israel out of Egypt. (Exod. 3: 9–10, NLT)

Action of faith:

> *It was by faith* that Moses left the land of Egypt, not fearing the king's anger. He kept right on going because he kept his eyes on the one who is invisible. (Heb. 11:27, NLT)

Do you see the pattern? An action of faith is the result of following a clear instruction from God. *It was by faith* that Noah, Abraham, and Moses received God's promises. Faith must go hand in hand with actions according to what we have *heard* from God.

Many people take action without seeking God's guidance. They act and then expect God to intervene. When everything goes wrong or when they don't get the desired outcome, they realize the action was never inspired by God.

God will lead an action of faith. Your job is to:

- *Pray* to seek the guidance of the Holy Spirit,
- *Wait* to hear His voice,
- *Receive* His instruction,
- *Take action* according to the instruction given to you.

Jesus spent hours in prayer daily. This was necessary so that he could hear the voice of His Father and act accordingly. The result of first *praying*, then *waiting*, then *receiving* an instruction and finally *acting* was powerful signs, miracles, and wonders. All of us have been called to have this kind of close relationship with God and walk under the guidance of the Holy Spirit. Wouldn't you like to see miracles and wonders in your love life? You need to walk in faith as God leads you.

What to expect when God calls you to take action

- *God's instruction might not match your plans.*

God's instruction will not always align with our plans, at least not right away. God's ways are higher and better than our ways (Isa. 55:8–9). Regardless of our ultimate destination, God will take us on a journey that requires surrender, patience, and perseverance on our part.

Remember the story I shared in the first chapter about my plans to leave my home and move to Canada? As exciting and appealing as this idea was, it was not inspired by the Holy Spirit. I didn't even know who the Holy Spirit was in that moment because I was a brand-new believer. Since I was so young in my faith, I didn't have spiritual maturity to seek God for such an important decision as this one. The plan to go to Canada was completely fueled by my will and desires, not God's.

God stopped me from continuing with my plans. His instruction was, "Stay, do not leave." Obviously, God's instruction was not at all what I wanted to hear or do! Most times when I receive instructions from God, they rarely match my plans or desires. In fact, they are often completely contrary to what I would rather do. When God calls you to action, be ready to surrender your plans and ways to follow His.

- *God's timing does not depend on your desire, resources, or circumstances even if you think the time is "right."*

Soon after surrendering my plans of going to Canada to God, He blessed me with the awesome job I described in the previous chapter. I was able to work from home, have a flexible schedule, earn a good salary, and have freedom to work remotely from anywhere I wanted.

I thought that God had given me that job so that I could leave home safely and carry on with my travel plans to Canada. After all, I could afford paying all my expenses and live anywhere while still keeping my job. Apparently, all the pieces were falling into place. I said, "This is the *right* time!" I thought God was finally opening the way for me to leave home.

Over the course of seven years, I tried to leave two times; and both times, God stopped me and showed me it wasn't His time yet. One obstacle after another got in my way: my parents were not supportive, my pastors were also in disagreement, and I had high student loans to pay.

Although I had the desire, resources, and suitable circumstances to carry out my plan, God was not leading me to take action. I had to keep on waiting until He gave me a green flag.

You too might feel tempted to make decisions based on what you think is the *right* time. Keep in mind that even if everything looks like it is, it might not be God's perfect timing yet.

Having the resources and suitable circumstances to carry out a plan or dream does not necessarily mean that God is calling you to take action. God imprints dreams in our hearts that might take a long time to come to fruition. This is especially true when it comes to finding a partner and getting married.

• *Not everybody is going to be excited or supportive about what God has spoken to you.*

In the Bible, Joseph was a man to whom God spoke in dreams from a very young age. In his dreams, God told him he would reign over his entire family. Joseph's parents and brothers didn't believe in the dreams that Joseph was having. Perhaps Joseph himself wondered why he was dreaming such things. However, God was speaking to Joseph's heart about the things that were to come.

If God has given you a dream or a vision about something, not everyone is going to be thrilled for you. Not everyone will believe in the dream God has given you. It happened to Joseph, and it happened to me too. Perhaps people, including those who love you the most, will try to convince you that what God has spoken to you is not true or that it will never happen. Do not be discouraged. If God really spoke to you, it will happen no matter what others think. Persevere in faith and be expectant about the fulfillment of His promise.

The day God called me to leave my comfort zone

Going back to my story, seven years after I surrendered my dream to God of going to Canada, He spoke to me again and said, "Cintia, the time has come for you to leave home. You are ready. I'll take you to a land that you do not know, and I will bless you there."

"Really, God!" I exclaimed. I couldn't fully grasp what I had just heard, but my heart jumped, full of excitement and expectation. However, the final destination was not going to be Canada as I thought, but another place that I didn't know.

Perhaps my dream of going to Canada was, after all, just a misinterpretation of the real dream God had imprinted in my heart since the day I was born. I mixed God's dream with my own, and the result was a distortion of the truth. After much prayer, God showed that the place He was sending me to was Austin, Texas.

I asked God how I could be sure I heard correctly from Him. I wanted to make sure it wasn't just another "great idea" I made up. If I was going to go to Austin, it had to be because God was sending me there. It was then that I prayed for several signs of confirmation:

- complete support and blessing of my parents,
- blessing of my pastors,
- financial provision and being debt free before I left. This included paying off student loans and car payment,
- being able to pay in advance all travel expenses including rent and transportation for my six months stay in Austin,
- at least $5,000 in savings in case something went wrong.

The confirmations I was asking for were not easy at all. If God really wanted me to leave my home, then a miracle was needed for these five things to come to pass. But God responded to my requests one by one, so I had no doubt that God's time had come and that Austin was the place to which He was sending me.

For the first time in seven years, my parents and pastors supported my plan of leaving home, and they had complete peace about my decision. This alone was the greatest confirmation for me! They all granted me their blessing without hesitation.

I packed two suitcases full of clothes; filled the gas tank of my car; and drove from Monterrey, Mexico, to Austin, Texas, in the spring of 2012. This was an *action of faith*.

I had never been in Austin before, neither did I know anybody there. However, as foreign as that city was to me, everything went very smoothly, and I felt settled right away. God provided a safe place for me to live with two young Christian ladies. He also led me to a church where He challenged my faith even more. But the most important thing God did during that trip was that He introduced me to my future husband.

It might sound pretty radical to leave home and go to another country as I did, but that was God's instruction for me. It does not mean that you have to do the same thing unless God is leading you to do so. It all depends on God's leading, and for that, it is necessary to seek His direction in prayer.

Actions of faith versus actions in the flesh

It seems exciting to leave your comfort zone, right? It sounds great to venture out and try something new. But what if God is not leading that action you are taking? Or what if it is not His timing yet? The line between walking under the guidance of the Holy Spirit and walking under the desires of our flesh may not always be clear. We need to be careful to follow the leading of the Spirit so that we can avoid the danger of following our flesh.

Despair over being single and wanting to have a relationship can lead many people to make hasty decisions. This is especially true for those that have been single for a very long time. Do not rush to make decisions based on your emotions; your flesh will end up leading you and not God.

An action inspired and initiated by God is an *action of faith*, whereas an action initiated by human will and emotions is an *action of the flesh*. Consider the differences between the two:

Love on Hold Actions of Faith versus Actions of the Flesh Comparison Table	
Action of Faith	Action of the Flesh
There is faith.	There is no faith.
It is started, inspired, and directed by the Holy Spirit.	It is started, inspired, and directed by human will, emotions, and feelings.

It requires seeking God's guidance and waiting to hear from Him.	There is no seeking of God. The action is taken based on emotions and self-interests.
God energizes this action. There is divine intervention.	God does not energize this action. It lacks the life of God.
It is an action done in God's time, with the right motive, to do it all for the glory of God.	It is an action made at the wrong time, and with the wrong motive, to satisfy personal desires.
It is based on a thought that was inspired by God, and it results in a blessing.	It is based on a "good idea" that comes from human will. However, it does not work.

The table above is summarized in the following scripture:

> Those who live according to the *flesh* have their minds set on what the *flesh desires;* but those who live in accordance with the *Spirit* have their minds set on what the *Spirit desires.* The mind governed by the flesh is death, but the mind governed by the Spirit is life and peace. (Rom. 8: 5–6, NIV)

Having a relationship with God gives us access to hearing His voice. He shows us through His Word and prayer what to do. It is very possible that His instruction is contrary to what you would rather do, but hang in there. If you follow His lead, the outcome will be far greater and better than what you imagined in your wildest dreams.

Have you heard God's voice correctly?

It is normal and actually very important to ask ourselves if we have heard correctly from God. The Bible says that God's voice is like a "gentle whisper" (1 Kings 19:12); it can be easily confused with our own thoughts. For this reason, it is very hard to listen to His voice if we do not quiet our minds and walk away for a moment from the distractions around us.

If you want to be sure that you've actually heard and received an instruction from God, you can ask Him for signs of confirmation. There is nothing wrong with asking God for confirmations to show us if what we thought we heard comes from Him.

Besides the signs that you will ask God, I will give you three important pieces of advice that will help you know that He is leading you:

1. *Any instruction given by God should not contradict His Word, the Bible.*

> We also have the prophetic message as something completely reliable, and you will do well to pay attention to it, as to a light shining in a dark place. (2 Pet. 1:19, NIV)

Nothing that God asks you to do is going to be against the principles and commands He has established in the Bible. The Bible is the most reliable prophetic word and was fully inspired by God. It is the most complete manual that you can base your life and decisions on.

In order to do this, you obviously need to know the Bible, meditate on it daily, and understand it. By becoming a member of a Bible-based church and by joining a community Bible study, you can learn how to read it and interpret it.

2. *Having the approval and blessing of your parents is a good sign of confirmation.*

> Honor your father and your mother, as the Lord your God has commanded you, so that you may live long and that it may go well with you

in the land the Lord your God is giving you.
(Deut. 5:16, NIV)

Looking for the counsel and direction of parents may sound awkward for some people. The spirit of independence is influencing the decisions of many, making it impossible for them to live under parental authority. This is especially true among singles.

If you are single, your parents are the authority that God has established over you. There is great power and blessing in walking under the direction, counsel, and instruction of your parents.

God honors and blesses those who honor their parents with their obedience; this is the first commandment with a promise. God will bless you and will open the way for you to obtain the promises He has given you to the extent that you respect their authority in your life.

If for any reason your parents cannot be your authority, you can seek spiritual covering, instruction, and direction from someone that lives under the lordship of Christ. It can be your pastor, a spiritual mentor, a church leader, or another member of your family. It has to be someone that can hold you accountable and someone from whom you can receive instruction and most importantly, correction.

3. *God's instruction will never require that you pursue a man that is not your husband.*

> Promise me, O women of Jerusalem, by the
> gazelles and wild deer, not to awaken love until
> the time is right. (Song of Sol. 2:7, NLT)

God will never, ever lead you to pursue a man in any capacity or form, unless that man is your husband. As women, we are quick to act based on emotions and feelings. Often, our tendency is to make things easier for the man that we are interested in. We think that we are the ones who must take the initiative: calling him first, inviting him to go out on a date, moving to a different town to be near him, living with him before marriage, asking him to propose to us, and the list goes on!

Women who pursue a man and make things easier for him will usually end up hurt, disappointed, or rejected because this goes against the order established by God. Do not deny a man the pleasure of pursuing you. He will appreciate you not pursuing him and will cherish you forever if he had to fight for winning your precious heart. If a man is not pursuing you nor fighting for you, you can remain assured that he is simply not your man.

In conclusion, if you are a single woman and you feel ready for marriage, ask God if there is anything new you can do in order to meet your future husband. For the most part, there are two instructions you can receive from God: He might say you don't need to do anything for now, or He might tell you that you need to walk in faith in the instruction He is going to give you. Both the waiting time and the taking an action of faith are extremely important and work together for God's purposes to be fulfilled in our lives.

If God has you in a season of waiting at this moment, do not rush to try to do things that He has not called you to do. Let the waiting season perform its work in you and in the man that God is preparing for you. Rest assured, the waiting season always comes to an end. Attune your ear to the Holy Spirit constantly. Ask Him if there is anything He wants you to do and when His timing is to begin. Once God calls you to walk in faith and take action, rejoice and get excited! It is time for you to leave your comfort zone. I guarantee you, once you leave, nothing will ever be the same. I pray that every action of faith you take in your journey to find love will get you closer to God and closer to meeting the love of your life on earth.

CHAPTER 13

DIVINE ENCOUNTER

After receiving the five confirmations I had prayed for, I left home to start the journey to my dream. I drove for nearly nine hours before I arrived in Austin. I did not know anybody there, but I wasn't worried about that. Knowing that God was leading my steps was enough for me to be at peace during the first few lonely days. During the first two weeks, I spent a good amount of time doing research about churches in the area. I came up with a list of five churches that I was planning to visit. On the third day, I visited the first church on my list. I didn't attend the Sunday service but a connect class they were hosting on Tuesday nights. I had no idea what God had in store for me that evening.

The class consisted of eight sessions, one session per week. Due to the time of my arrival, I missed the first session, but I attended the second. When I entered that room, there were about fifty people and several round tables with ten chairs each. I sat in the first seat I saw available and waited for the session to start.

After a few minutes, a young woman came up behind me and touched my shoulder. "Excuse me, in what part of Austin do you live?" she asked.

"On Riverside," I answered.

"Oh, you live in South Austin. We are sitting people according to the area where they live—north, south, east, and west. You are seated in the table of the north. Come, let me take you to the South Austin table."

I just shrugged my shoulders and followed her as she directed me where to sit.

I didn't know why she had randomly touched my shoulder. I mean, there were so many people there; how did she notice me? I had no idea that her simple act of touching my shoulder and leading me to a new table would change my life forever. Sometimes, I even wonder if it was an angel on assignment sent by God. If that was indeed the case, I will never know.

At the South Austin table, there were already nine people sitting and only one seat available, mine. I took my seat and smiled at everyone. By the time this happened, most tables were already full and the presenter took the microphone and welcomed everyone. He asked us to spend a few minutes introducing ourselves to the people around our table.

Silence was immediately broken with the voices of all the people in the room connecting with each other. At my table, people began to introduce themselves one by one. They shared their names and details about their jobs, how long they had been attending church, and what brought them to the class. Some of these people had been attending this church for months, and a few others had for years. First Bud spoke, then Alicia, then Heather, and all the others until it was Caleb's turn, the guy sitting next to me.

Caleb said he had been attending that church for almost two years and that he always sat in the back row of church. He also said that he was the first guy to leave after service and had never connected with anyone. The reason he had come to the connect class was because he thought it was finally time to take the next step and get involved and meet some people.

Once he finished his presentation, I didn't say anything but thought, *Wow, seriously? Two years in church and not involved or connected? No bueno!* I thought that was pretty awkward, but at least he was now on the right path to getting involved.

After Caleb, it was my turn. I said something like, "Hello, everyone. My name is Cintia. I'm from Mexico, and this is my third day in Austin. The reason I came to this class is because I am looking for a church to join, and I decided to come to this class to learn more about this one."

My brief presentation raised a few eyebrows and curiosity among the others.

"How did you know about this class if you have only been in Austin three days?" They asked.

"I did some research and found out about this class online just a few days ago," I answered.

"Did you come to Austin all by yourself?"

"Yep, I actually drove from Mexico to Austin by myself in my own car."

"Wow, you drove? How courageous! Do you know anyone here? Any friends or family?"

"No, I don't know anyone. You are, in fact, the first people I have met and spoken with in the last three days," I said laughing.

"And what brought you to Austin?" They asked.

"God," I answered.

"God?" They were puzzled.

The dialogue continued for a few more minutes until the presenter interrupted and said it was time to start the session. I didn't know it at the time, but Caleb was very intrigued and wanted to know more about this adventurous Mexican who drove all by herself to Austin.

At the end of the session, the Holy Spirit revealed to me that this was not the church I was going to be a part of. So that was the first class I attended and the only one. In the following weeks, I continued my research, and I visited other churches until I found my Austin church home.

Before I said goodbye to the group, Caleb asked me for my phone number. I gave it to him and he gave me his. Very kindly, he walked me to my car. As he opened up the door of my car, he said, "This is a very dangerous city for a young lady like you. Be very careful. If you need help with anything, please do not hesitate to text me or call me. I'd love to help you."

In that moment, I knew that Caleb was interested in me, but my mind and heart were far from thinking about boys. I had so much stuff to figure out in Austin: getting to know the city, finding a church, making new friends, etc. Besides, I had decided not to start any love relationship until I was one-hundred percent sure that the next man I would date was the man that God had chosen to be my husband. What I did not know was that God, in fact, had prepared that connect class, assigned that person who touched my shoulder, and reserved that one empty seat at the South Austin table to prepare a divine encounter that night.

God did not create love for it to be so hard to find

Almost every single woman dreams of two moments in her life: the day she will find love and the day she will get married. Some women spend years of their lives looking for love, only to be hurt and to suffer disappointment after disappointment. I was one of those women. I wanted love in my life; I tried a lot of things to find Mr. Right and failed miserably. Men came into my life and left. Relationships that quickly started also quickly ended. One day among tears and with much frustration, I said to God, "God, I can't believe You made love to be this hard! Why, if I have given my best, have I not been able to find it?" God remained silent.

When God remains silent, it is because He is working in our hearts. He is touching the deepest part of our being and transforming it. That day, God was healing my heart and bringing me to a moment of complete surrender. God was asking me to surrender my desire for a husband.

With so much brokenness, I set before God this longing of my heart. I still wanted to find love, but I had given up its pursuit. I had been pursuing love for years without success. Obviously, my approach was not sufficient because it hadn't worked at all. I needed God's intervention; I realized this matter was completely out of my control.

I decided to focus my attention on God and pursue His love instead of the love of a man. I stopped looking for love because that was consuming me emotionally; it was stressful, debilitating, and frustrating. I decided to let God bring it when He wanted if it was His will to bless me with a husband. I no longer wanted to be in control of my situation, but instead wanted God to be. These decisions became the perfect preface for God to intervene and prepare a divine encounter with the man who would be my husband.

Divine encounters are real and are not just limited to biblical times. The desire of God is to always be the protagonist of each love story and to originate a divine encounter for each of His children with their future spouse. God wants to get all the glory in your love life, just as He got all the glory in the life of several single women of the Bible such as Esther, Ruth, Rebekah, and Rachel. Let's take a look at some of the divine encounters in the Bible and how God miraculously intervened for these to happen.

The divine encounters of the Bible

The Bible reveals details of God's divine intervention to introduce several single women to the men that would be their husbands. We can learn from the supernatural encounters between Isaac and Rebekah, Jacob and Rachel, and Ruth and Boaz. Stories like these leave modern, single women sighing and longing for their own love story.

All of these women found themselves in God's appointed place and time to cross paths with the men destined to be their husbands. The stories tell amazing details of how God intervened to make these encounters possible. Although all of these encounters were planned and originated by God, it was necessary that these people had faith and obeyed the instruction that God gave them.

The resulting marriages of each of these love stories had great impact in future generations. God honored the faith and obedience of these women and their husbands by blessing them with children who would carry out great deeds and mark the history of mankind forever. For example, the sons of Rebekah and Ruth were ancestors of Jesus and are within His genealogy. The son of Rachel was greatly used by God to save the lives of thousands, including the people of Israel.

God has a great purpose for your marriage also. This purpose is eternal and goes beyond anything you can think, imagine, or understand. How do you know if your future marriage will be greatly used by God to bring salvation to many? Or if your children will be future influential leaders that will change history? You do not know! But God knows, and He has His purposes already prepared. *If you honor God with your faith and wait for Him to bring your husband, He will honor you with a godly man, and your children will be part of His holy nation.*

Let us now see how the divine encounters of the Bible took place in the life of Rebekah, Rachel, and Ruth.

Isaac and Rebekah
(Read Gen. 24)

The Rebekah of the Bible is an example of a hardworking woman with a servant's heart. Her name in Hebrew means "woman of captivating beauty." She lived in the city of Nahor in Aram while Isaac, the man that she married, lived in Canaan. Given the geographical distance between these two people, the encounter between Isaac and Rebekah cannot be explained other than by divine intervention.

For Abraham, Isaac's father, it was important to find a good wife for his son, a woman of God. Abraham didn't want a Canaanite for Isaac because the Canaanites were idolaters, and they worshiped other gods. Instead, he wanted a wife from his own country for his son. Abraham sent his servant to seek a wife for Isaac in the land of Nahor in Aram where his relatives lived. He told him that the angel of God would go before him to prosper his journey. The servant began the journey, taking ten camels with him.

The distance between Aram and Canaan was about five hundred miles, a journey that would take about a month when traveled by camel. I can't imagine what it was like for Abraham's servant to do such a long and exhausting trip under the hot sun, crossing mountainous terrain. However, this story illustrates that for God, distance and geographical location is not a limitation to bring two people together.

The servant finally arrived at a well outside the city of Nahor where the daughters of the townspeople came to draw water. Thirsty and exhausted, the servant asked for a sign from God to know if any of these women would be the one God had chosen as a wife for Isaac. He prayed:

> See, I am standing beside this spring. If a young woman comes out to draw water and I say to her, "Please let me drink a little water from your jar," and if she says to me, 'Drink, and I'll draw water for your camels too,' let her be the one the Lord has chosen for my master's son." Before I finished praying in my heart, Rebekah came out, with her jar on her shoulder. She went down to the spring and drew water, and I said to her, "Please give me a drink." (Gen. 24:43–45, NIV)

Notice that the servant did not pray for a woman of good looks, or pleasant personality; although all these are very desirable qualities and Rebekah had them all. No. He prayed for a woman willing to serve; in other words, he prayed for a woman with a *servant's heart*.

Rebekah saw a need that she could meet, and she immediately went down to the spring, filled her jar, and came up again. She not only gave water to the servant but she offered to give water to all the camels as well. For the record, a thirsty camel can consume up to two hundred liters of water. Can you imagine how many times Rebekah had to fill her jar to give water to ten camels? Let's suppose the jar had a capacity of five liters. If this was the case, Rebekah had to fill it up forty times to serve one camel. Possibly, these camels did not drink two hundred liters that day, but you get the point. It took a lot of trips to the well to do the job.

This attitude of service was the confirmation for which the servant had prayed. God rewarded the kind, humble, and generous heart of Rebekah by choosing her to be Isaac's wife. Rebekah's parents met with Abraham's servant and heard the story. They realized that all of this was coming from God, so they blessed their daughter, and Rebekah agreed to travel to Canaan to meet with Isaac. The Bible tells us that Isaac took Rebekah as his wife, and he loved her.

The story of Isaac and Rebekah reflects God's intervention to bring together two people who lived in different lands but who shared the same faith. Usually, nobody marries without knowing the other person first. We may think that the decision of Isaac and Rebekah to get married without knowing each other was quite risky. However, by the time they knew they were going to be husband and wife, God had already worked in supernatural ways and showed clear confirmations that this encounter had been orchestrated by Him. Quite possibly, God also prepared the hearts of Isaac and Rebekah for them to experience a *love at first sight.* For this reason, the marriage of Isaac and Rebekah was a marriage of faith. Faith in God who had prepared all the previous events so that they could come face to face with each other and unite their lives forever.

Jacob and Rachel
(Read Gen. 29)

The Rachel of the Bible was a woman with a humble heart. Her name in Hebrew means, "The Lamb of God." Rachel lived in Paddan Aram while Jacob, who was the son of Isaac and Rebekah, lived in Canaan. The love story of Jacob and Rachel resembles in many ways the story of Isaac and Rebekah. Just as Abraham sought for his son Isaac a wife from his land and relatives, so Isaac advised his son Jacob to follow in the same steps. Isaac told Jacob not to marry a Canaanite woman but to go to the land of Paddan Aram and to find there a woman from the daughters of his uncle Laban.

In both stories, we can see that for Abraham and Isaac, it was important that their children did not join a Canaanite woman because they worshiped other gods. Therefore, to marry one of them was to be *unequally yoked.*

Following his father's instructions, Jacob traveled to Paddan Aram where he encountered a well where there were shepherds taking care of flocks of sheep. Jacob greeted them and asked if they knew Laban, his uncle. As he was talking to them, Rachel, who was the daughter of Laban, came to water her father's sheep for she was a shepherd (Gen. 29:9–10).

Rachel was at her father's service, taking care of his sheep. It was no coincidence that Rachel went to water her sheep at the same time that Jacob arrived at the well for every event had been prepared by God to create a divine encounter between them.

In his book, *All the Women of the Bible,* Herbert Lockyer describes this moment as follows:

> That meeting between Jacob and Rachel was of God, and it was His providence that ordered the first glimpse of each other at the well. We are apt to forget that often the most seemingly ordinary incidents in life are as much of the divine plan as the smallest parts of a watch, and upon these smallest parts of the plan all the others depend. Our steps, when ordered by the Lord, lead to great issue. As far as Jacob and Rachel were concerned, that meeting was unforeseen and unpremeditated.[18]

Jacob was so captivated by Rachel's beauty that he fell in love with her when he first saw her. Rachel was doing just what was expected of her at the time, taking care of her father's sheep. What Rachel was doing is a representation of what God, our Father, expects His daughters to do—to take care of His sheep. The sheep of God are your brothers and sisters in Christ. They are the sick and the needy; the ones who are overlooked and unfortunate. They are those people who do not know God yet, but whom God wants to reach through

---

[18] Lockyer, Herbert. *All the Women of the Bible,* Zondervan, Oct. 3, 1988. *BibleGateway,* http://www.zondervan.com/all-the-women-of-the-Bible. Accessed April 3, 2018.

you. Just as Rachel was at her father's service taking care of his sheep, so God wants us to take care of his flock.

Rachel was doing *God's work* when He introduced her to her husband. When we are about our Heavenly Father's service, taking care of what matters most to Him, He takes care of every single need of our heart and soul.

Boaz and Ruth
(Read Ruth 1–4)

The Ruth of the Bible is a loyal woman, willing to sacrifice herself for others. Her name in Hebrew means, "faithful companion and friend." Ruth lived with her mother-in-law Naomi, who was a widow and had two sons: Mahlon, who was married to Ruth; and Kilion, who was married to Orpah. Both Mahlon and Kilion died, leaving Ruth and Orpah as widows under Naomi's care.

Since Ruth and Orpah were still very young, Naomi thought they could remarry and live their lives with another man. So she encouraged them to return to their mother's home and told them:

> May the Lord grant that each of you will
> find rest in the home of another husband.
> (Ruth 1:9, NIV)

Orpah and Ruth did not accept Naomi's suggestion. However, after Naomi insisted, Orpah kissed her mother-in-law goodbye, but Ruth clung to her.

Orpah probably thought that Naomi's suggestion was the best thing she could do for herself if she wanted to find happiness again with a new husband. After all, what kind of future could she have next to an old woman like Naomi? What kind of dreams and aspirations could she have if she stayed in poverty, without a man that could provide for her?

However, Ruth did not think of herself. She had unconditional love for Naomi, and it was more important for her to take care of her mother-in-law than to look for a man to remarry.

> But Ruth replied, "Don't urge me to leave
> you or to turn back from you. Where you go I
> will go, and where you stay I will stay. Your peo-
> ple will be my people and your God my God."
> (Ruth 1:16, NIV)

Here, you have Ruth and Orpah, two young ladies who experienced the same tragedy of losing their husbands and facing an uncer-
tain future. Both were presented with the same opportunity to return
home to find a husband and remarry, but they choose differently.
Orpah's decision was based on pursuing her own personal interests
while Ruth gave up the possibility of remarrying and decided to stay
with Naomi and take care of her.

Not knowing what the future might hold, Ruth left her father,
mother, and homeland, and went with Naomi to Bethlehem, trusting that God would provide for them. Ruth knew her mother-in-law
was old and had no strength to work, so she assumed responsibility
for taking care of her and working to provide food for both of them.

The story tells us that Ruth went out to the fields to pick up
leftover grain. It turned out that she entered a field belonging to
Boaz, a relative of Elimelek, Naomi's deceased husband.

It was no mere coincidence that Ruth walked right into the field
of one of Elimelek's relatives for God had previously planned this
very moment. God led Ruth to go and work precisely in that field
because He had a very special plan for this young lady, to meet the
man that would be her future husband.

God prepared a divine encounter between Ruth and Boaz. This
encounter occurred while she was picking up grain from the field. It
is possible that Ruth's beauty initially grabbed Boaz's attention, and
he felt immediately attracted to her, but the Bible leaves no record
of this. If that was the case, Boaz always showed a respectful attitude toward Ruth and did not pursue her, but rather helped her and
allowed her to work at his field. This attitude of Boaz is worthy of a
man of God, a man who knows how to respect a woman and who
does not act based on emotional impulses or mere physical attrac-

tion. Boaz respected Ruth at all times, and provided protection and provision for her and her mother-in-law.

The Bible leaves a record of at least three qualities of Ruth that grabbed Boaz's attention:

- her *faithfulness* toward her mother-in-law Naomi (Ruth 2:11a),
- her *courage* demonstrated when she left everything behind to follow Naomi (Ruth 2:11b, NIV).
- her *hardworking* attitude and willingness to serve others (Ruth 2:5–7).

Ruth had unknowingly gained the admiration of Boaz, and for this reason, he called her a "virtuous woman" (Ruth 3:11, NLT). Her beauty, servant's heart, faithfulness, courage, and sacrificial love for Naomi captivated Boaz's heart.

Since Boaz was a relative of Naomi's deceased husband Elimelek, he was in a position to redeem Ruth and his mother-in-law. Then they got married, and the Lord enabled Ruth to conceive and give birth to a son (Ruth 4:13).

Ruth never imagined that she would end up being the wife of such a godly, respectable, and influential man, let alone give birth to a child who would be an ancestor of our Savior. Perhaps Ruth imagined that widowhood would be her condition for the rest of her life. Yet God had different plans.

This inspiring story illustrates the hope that many women of today who are widows or have gone through divorce can have when they put their trust in God. God has the power to change your circumstances and bless you with a godly husband if getting married again is a longing of your heart.

What we can learn from Rebekah, Rachel, and Ruth?

In the above three stories, we can see a common denominator—God led each of these women to the right place at the right time to have a divine encounter with their future husband. They did not plan it. None of them was actively seeking a husband when these encounters took place. Most likely, they all had dreamed of getting married one day. However, the blessing of finding a husband did not come about because of their efforts but instead came about through the intervention of God.

One thing we can learn from Rebekah, Rachel, and Ruth is that these three women all had a *servant's heart.* They were all working and serving others in the moment God introduced them to their husbands.

If you delight in the things of God, He will take care of the desires of your heart. If you serve God with your time, your talent, your abilities, and you do it with a sincere and loving heart, God is going to bless you.

The divine encounter that God has prepared for your life will happen when you least expect it. It is important that you ask God for discernment and wisdom to recognize your husband when God puts him before you. Meanwhile, focus on serving God and serving others out of love for God.

May your character reflect the character of Christ—and be full of love, gentleness, kindness, generosity, faithfulness, humility, obedience, and sacrifice—as it was with the characters of Rebekah, Rachel, and Ruth.

God has purposes already prepared for you

God has already prepared times, places, people, and circumstances for us to fulfill His plans and purposes. If we seek His direction, sooner or later, we will intersect the paths that He has prepared for us. When we intersect one of God's paths, supernatural and miraculous things happen.

I am convinced that many people and circumstances I encountered in my life were planned and orchestrated by God so that I would meet the man who would be my husband. The place I was born, the school where I studied, the year I studied abroad, the job I got, the relationships I had, my trip to Austin, my decision to attend that connect class; everything, absolutely everything, aligned for this divine encounter to take place.

Caleb was the man God brought into my life to be my husband. Everything was smooth and beautiful because God had originated a divine encounter between us. When God orchestrates your story, love is not tormenting, difficult, or forced. Instead, it is beautiful, pleasant, and exciting.

Believe that God is preparing a divine encounter with the man who will be your husband. It is possible that God will blind the eyes of men that are not meant to be part of your life. They are going to be blinded by God's glory shining through you, and they will not be able to see anything else. It is likely that relationships you start with these men will not work, and those who initially were interested in you might suddenly lose interest. Don't get discouraged if you see this happening. It might be the very hand of God making those men walk away. He is protecting you from ending up with the wrong person.

But the right man, the one that God has chosen for you, will be able to recognize and see you for what He has created you to be. That man will love you and cherish you. Embrace this promise with faith for as God did with Rebekah, Rachel, Ruth, and me, He will also do for you. I hope you rise as a woman of faith and that you start praying for a divine encounter, one that occurs when you might least expect it, but in the perfect timing of God.

CHAPTER 14

I Didn't Know He Was Going to Be My Husband

It was only two weeks since I had met Caleb for the first time in that connection class. He invited me out to have dinner, and I accepted. That night, we enjoyed a great conversation as we had a glass of wine at a local restaurant in South Austin. Caleb was very curious about me. He had a lot of questions, and I enjoyed that. He was attentive, was a good listener, and was very fun to be with. He seemed to be a very smart guy just by the way he talked. We got along well from the beginning; I enjoyed his company and thought we could become good friends.

A week later, we got together again to celebrate St. Patrick's Day with some of his friends; this was the second time we hung out. That night, we had a blast! I noticed that he was very protective—always looking after me, always asking if I was okay or if I needed anything.

At the end of the evening, he drove me back home. Once we arrived, he parked; and when I was ready to say goodbye and get out of the car, he looked into my eyes and made an important declaration. "Cintia, I think God brought you to Austin to meet me."

I was baffled. "Why do you think that?" I asked.

Then he said, "I have been praying for a wife, a helper, a godly woman. I think it is you whom I have been praying for. I think God brought you to Austin to meet me because you're going to be my wife."

I could not believe what Caleb said. It was only our second time together! He did not know me well enough. How could he be so sure of something like that? For a moment, I paused as I digested his words. He had a lot of great qualities that I was looking for. First of all, he was a believer; to me, that was the most important thing. Second, he was smart, respectful, attentive, and fun, and had a successful career. Third, he had very good looks. He was tall, had blue eyes, and he was very fit. Those were all good reasons to be excited about starting a relationship with him, but it was too soon. We had just met, and he was still a stranger to me. Furthermore, I had always pictured in my mind I would marry a pastor, and he wasn't one. I couldn't move beyond the idea of being more than just friends at that moment.

"Umm, I don't know about that. I don't think so," I replied hesitantly.

Then he asked, "Well, could you pray so that God reveals to you His will about me?"

"Sure. I will," I said.

I gave him a hug and smiled. I said goodbye and stepped out of the car. Although I had told him I would pray about it, I didn't. I was convinced that Caleb and I were just meant to be friends and nothing else.

For many years, I had created in my mind a *model* of the man that I wanted as a husband. I had been praying about it fervently. My prayers were for a man who was a pastor or evangelist. In practical terms, if a man who pursued me was not behind a pulpit preaching on a Sunday, I immediately thought, *This is not the one. God has a pastor for me.*

I had truly believed that God had called me to be the wife of a pastor. Men who did not fit this model were immediately thrown off my radar. Caleb did not seem to be the man I had been praying for.

God blinded my eyes temporarily

During the next five months, Caleb and I continued to hang out as friends. Although I did not see Caleb as the man who would be my future husband, he never lost his conviction that I was the woman God had brought to be his wife. He was so confident about it and persevered. He accepted my pace without putting any pressure on me. He did not get upset if I did not accept an invitation to go out, he didn't get offended if I did not answer the phone when he called me, he didn't give up when I told him I just wanted to be friends. But all that time, he was trying to conquer my heart. I am convinced that his battlefield was in the secret place—alone with God in prayer, for God to change my thoughts and feelings about him.

A few years before I met Caleb, there was a time when I was very heartbroken because of a relationship that did not work. That relationship was actually with a man who met the criteria I had been praying for. I was deeply attracted to him and so convinced that he was the man God had brought to my life to be my husband. Oh, what a great disappointment that relationship was! The six months I was in that relationship were the most emotionally devastating of my entire life as a single woman!

He was not a bad person; we were just unable to make each other happy no matter how hard we tried. We didn't seem to be compatible even though we were attracted to each other. We wanted things to work out, but they didn't. I think the only thing that kept us together those six months was physical attraction, but other than that, the relationship was very empty. God allowed me to temporarily get exactly what I wanted, just to hit the wall and realize that many times, what we ask for is not the best thing for us and will not make us happy.

After that relationship ended, I cried out to God and prayed for Him to spiritually blind my eyes when He brought the man who would be my husband:

> Lord, when you bring my husband to my
> life, do not let me recognize him right away.

169

Please blind my eyes in order to protect my heart and my feelings. But let him know that I am the woman you have destined for him so that he fights for me. And once I'm ready and he's in love with me, then open my eyes again and let me see him for who he is and let me fall in love with him.

I did not expect that prayer to be honored and answered, but it was! God blinded my eyes temporarily. He put a veil over my eyes so that I could not recognize Caleb as my husband until the time God had appointed. During this time of blindness, God worked in both of us, shaping our character and faith. What God did during that time of blindness would never have been possible had I started an immediate love relationship with Caleb.

I think that God will blind the eyes of many singles so they cannot recognize their husband or wife immediately. God will do this when He considers them not yet ready to date or get married. One reason I believe God does this is because He first prepares the heart of each person so they are able to cherish and love their future spouse in a godly way. After God finishes His work and considers them ready, He removes the veil for them to be able to recognize each other as the spouse God has provided.

A revealing love letter

Caleb and I continued to be friends during my time in Austin. My staying in Austin lasted five months; after which, I had to go back to Mexico. The day before I left, I started packing, and Caleb came to help me. That day, he gave me a letter that read as follows:

Dear Cintia,

What an amazing impact you have already had on my life!

170

When I signed up for that church's connect class, I had no idea the connection that would be made there—truly a blessing! As soon as I met you, I was captivated. You had a presence, a gleam, a beauty that I wanted to share more time with. I know now that was the Holy Spirit and God's love shining through you.

You had a conviction to follow God when He sent you to Austin, and even though you didn't know exactly why you were sent here, He does! He sent you to challenge you, inspire you . . . and you know what's next, to meet me! ☺

I have been praying for God to provide me a helper, one that He has set out for me from the beginning of creation. And although I don't know exactly what is next, He does.

I have faith that He will continue to lead both of us to fulfill the plans that He has. He is the maker of the puzzle that we operate in. And just as He says in Jeremiah 29:11—He has plans for us to prosper, and I have faith in His plan!

Even though we have just begun to know each other, there is one thing I know, I want to know you more! I want to meet your father, your family and your pastor. I want to continue our conversations and continue to eat sushi with you.

Cintia, you are amazing. Your heart is filled with God's love. A great encourager and determined. I am so glad and blessed you came into my life and I look forward to the next chapter.

For His Glory and in His love,
Caleb

I read his letter in silence as he was right next to me. I was wowed and flattered by his words, but I did not know what to say when I finished reading them. My opinion about him had not changed; I still saw him only as a good friend. But I was surprised by his perseverance and his conviction that there would be something more between us. His commitment and determination were starting to get my attention. Caleb was not a man who would waste my time; he was ready to be a husband and make me his wife. I knew that if I agreed to be his girlfriend, it would not be too long before he proposed to me in marriage. I liked his attitude and readiness, but at the same time, this made me nervous. I did not see him the way he looked at me; he was convinced that I was the wife for whom he had been praying.

After I finished reading his letter I smiled, hugged him, and thanked him. Although I knew that Caleb was a great man, my eyes were still blinded. My heart was still closed to the idea of having romantic feelings for him. Perhaps God was already trying to tell me that Caleb was meant to be more than just a friend in my life, but I was very stubborn.

I finished packing that day, I gave Caleb a hug, and I got into my car. He got into his and followed me from behind for a few minutes until I took the road that would take me back to my country, and he took the road that would take him back to his home. I waved my hand out the window, saying goodbye, and he did the same. Our cars gradually distanced themselves until we lost sight of each other.

Paradigm shift

Two weeks after my departure, Caleb was boarding a plane whose destination was Monterrey, Mexico. He had decided to come visit me, firmly convinced that I was the love of his life.

Caleb's perseverance and determination were things that I really admired about him. However, my conviction that God would bless me with a pastor as a husband was, until that moment, unshakable. After all, who could have put such a desire in my heart but God himself? And if God had put such a desire, didn't He have the power to fulfill it? I was sure that my desire was holy, divinely inspired, and I was not willing to settle for anything other than what I considered God's calling for my life—to be a pastors' wife.

It happened that on Caleb's visit to Monterrey, my pastor met him, and they found a moment to talk. I did not know what their conversation had been about. When I asked Caleb, he just referred to it as a man-to-man conversation, and that was all.

I was curious to find out more about this mysterious conversation. Once Caleb left, I called my pastor on the phone. I never imagined that this phone call would set a new course to my life. The conversation went something like this.

———— ∞ ————

Me: "Good morning, Pastor Eduardo! How are you? This is Cintia."

Pastor: "Cintia, hello mija! Nice to hear from you. I am doing well. How can I help you?"

Me: "Pastor, Caleb told me that he had a conversation with you this weekend. I just wanted to know, what did you think about him?"

Pastor: "I think Caleb is a very good man. He's nice and very humble. We had a very good talk. Why?"

Me: "Well, I was curious to know, what did you talk about?"

Pastor: "Ah, okay. Caleb approached me for advice."

Me: "Advice? What kind of advice, Pastor?"

Pastor: "First, let me ask you a question, Cintia."

Me: "Yes."

Pastor: "Who is Caleb for you?"

Me: "Umm, he is a good friend. Why?"

Pastor: "Because he does not see you just as a friend. No man travels to another country to see a woman just to pursue a friendship. He has asked me for advice because he told me that he wants to start a relationship with you."

Me: "Yes, Pastor. I know he wants me to be his girlfriend and to become his wife, but I do not feel the same. I do not think that he is the man that God has chosen to be my husband."

Pastor: "Why do you think that, Cintia?"

Me: "Well, for many years, I have been praying for a pastor, a man who has a call to ministry. I would like to be a pastor's wife."

Pastor: "Ah, okay."

Me: "And Caleb is not that kind of man. He loves God, seeks God, has a relationship with God, but he is not a pastor."

Pastor: "Cintia, what you have asked God is very good, and who knows, maybe that's what He has in store for you. But I think it is time for you to surrender your paradigms to the Holy Spirit."

Me: "To surrender what?"

Pastor: "Your paradigms. That is, the concepts that you have created in your mind about the man that God has for you."

Me: "Pastor, do you think I have been wrong about what I have been praying for all this time?"

Pastor: "No, I do not know. Only the Spirit of God can reveal that to you, not me. Cintia, ask the Holy Spirit to completely break your paradigms. I want to encourage you to start asking God to show you the heart of Caleb and if He has any plans for you both. My wife and I will also be praying for you so that God reveals His will about this matter."

—— ♥♥ ——

The conversation with my pastor left me thinking a lot. His words were spinning in my head over and over again. "*It's time for you to surrender your paradigms to the Holy Spirit.*" Had I been praying wrong for years? Had the desire to marry a pastor not been placed by God in my heart after all? I was very confused.

I immediately felt the urge to seek God in prayer. Maybe the blessing of God was in front of my eyes, and I had not wanted to see it. Maybe I was so focused on getting what I wanted that I had forgotten to let God show me what He wanted for me.

I locked myself in my bedroom and prayed. I asked God to forgive me if I had been selfish, praying for a man according to my fleshly desires and not according to His perfect will. I surrendered to God my expectations about looks, profession, personality, age, etc. I asked God to break all these concepts and ideas I had created in my mind for years about the man I wanted for a husband. I desperately wanted Him to illuminate my understanding so that I could see His plan.

"Lord, show me Caleb's heart. If he is the man you have for me, please allow me to see him no longer as a friend but as my future husband. If he is the husband you are bringing to my life, let me feel that kind of romantic love for him. If it really is him, put your love in me to love him as you want me to love him," I prayed.

God remained silent; I did not hear Him say anything at all. He did not give any instruction or revelation. But the Holy Spirit began to touch my heart until I experienced complete breakthrough. I knew that in that moment, God was demolishing pride, selfishness, and wrong motives of my heart.

Deceitful paradigms

A *paradigm* is a model to follow. It is a group of concepts that we create in our mind about how we want something or someone to be. There are many types of paradigms on which we can base our choice for a partner, including physical appearance, personality, lifestyle, age, interests, spirituality, profession, culture, nationality, financial position, etc.

For example, a successful, career-driven woman may have created the paradigm that her future husband must have a successful career too and receive a higher salary than hers. Another single woman may have created the paradigm that her future husband must be within a certain age range. In my case, I created the paradigm that my husband had to be a pastor.

There are endless types of paradigms such as those related to height, body type, skin color, race, type of job, etc. All these are examples of models that single people create in their minds of what they believe is desirable, attractive, and acceptable. I have found that the older a person gets, the more paradigms and requirements they have about who they want to marry. This makes finding love a very complicated task.

These paradigms, if not fully inspired by the Holy Spirit, can be very deceitful and even dangerous. They have the power to completely deviate a person from God's plan. They can make someone end up with the wrong person or remain single for life, unable to find love.

What are the paradigms you have formed about your future husband? Take a few seconds to think about this question. Think of the physical, professional, and spiritual attributes you've been looking for as well as personality traits. Now imagine that God introduces you to a man who does not quite fit the criteria you have been looking for. Maybe that man doesn't look the way you imagined, or is much younger or older than you expected, or does not seem to have the kind of personality you are attracted to. Do you think you could recognize that man as the husband God is bringing to your life? Do you think you could trust God's wisdom more than yours?

Your argument may be, "Well, God knows my desires. He will not give me someone that wouldn't make me happy." In that argument, you are absolutely right! However, perhaps what you want versus what will really make you happy may be completely different things, and you don't even know it. But God does. God will not give you what you want but what He knows you need. He will bring a person that will complement you perfectly and that will help you become the woman and wife He has called you to be.

> The heart is deceitful above all things and beyond cure. Who can understand it? "I the Lord search the heart and examine the mind, to reward each person according to their conduct, according to what their deeds deserve." (Jer. 17:9–10, NIV)

The Bible says that our heart is extremely deceitful; it can deceive us and deviate us from God's plan. What we desire and expect to find in our future spouse may seem good to us but may be far from actually bringing good into our lives. Only God knows our heart and knows what we need. Only He knows the deepest desires of our soul. He will not give us our desires unless they are aligned to His will.

I think that the most important thing that every single believer should look for in his or her future spouse is spiritual compatibility.

Being *unequally yoked* can be detrimental for the success of any love relationship and marriage. Beyond spiritual compatibility, any other expectation should be surrendered to God. Would you be willing to say, "Lord, this is what I want, but not my will but yours be done"?

There will be times when God guides us through paths that are very different from what we had envisioned. In the end, we will find that His ways will always be better than ours. He will give us what we really need, what is good for us, what will fulfill the deepest longings of our soul (Jer. 29:11).

Get ready for God to change your paradigms

After Caleb had that conversation with my pastor, I started to pray for God to reveal what His plans were regarding Caleb and me. My parents and pastors joined me in prayer. After three weeks, God removed the veil from my eyes. I was able to see Caleb for who he was—the man God had chosen to be my husband. It was then that a prophetic word that had been given to me the previous year was fulfilled:

> When I (God) bring to you the man that is right, you are going to be blinded by the crown that he wears. But he is going to get your attention, and you are going to know that he is the one, and that he comes from my hand.

I had no more doubts about it. Caleb was going to be my husband! I had a complete feeling of peace, joy, and excitement.

I thought the desire of marrying a pastor had been placed by God in my heart. For that reason, I was determined to wait for God to respond to my request. I prayed for it many years, thinking that God was leading me to pray that way. Today, I understand that the reason I was praying that way was because the husband that God had in store for me was going to have a shepherd's heart.

Caleb leads me to the truth and the love of God at all times. He comforts my soul and leads me to green pastures in times of trouble.

He is a man of prayer, a man who cares for other people. He is the kind of man that would lay down his life for the sheep (John 10:11). Although he doesn't have a pastor's name in any church, he is the pastor of our household. My friend and editor Suzanne Zucca said, "Our God is so amazing, and He just never fits in the boxes of our small imaginations!"

We need to surrender to God our paradigms. Not everything that we think is best for us is necessarily the will of God for our lives or the way the blessing is going to be presented to us. *Many times, we can be so sure of what we want and so focused on getting it that we miss seeing what God is actually doing and wants to give us.*

When God sent the prophet Samuel to look for a man who was going to be the successor of King Saul, He said, "I am sending you to Jesse of Bethlehem. I have chosen one of his sons to be king" (1 Sam. 16:1b, NIV). Jesse had eight sons. When Samuel came to Jesse's house, Samuel saw Eliab, the oldest son of Jesse. Quite possibly, Eliab was a man with a strong body. Perhaps he was tall, handsome, with the right looks to be king. For when Samuel saw him, he thought, "Surely, this is the Lord's anointed" (1 Sam. 16:6). Samuel had created a paradigm about what the appearance of the future king chosen by God was going to be. But observe in the following scripture what God said to Samuel:

> Do not consider his *appearance* or his *height*, for I have rejected him. The Lord does not look at the things people look at. People look at *the outward appearance,* but the Lord looks at *the heart.* (1 Sam. 16:7, NIV)

After looking at all of Jesse's sons, God revealed to Samuel that the youngest son, the shortest, a young boy of fair skin and red hair named David would be the new king. David had neither the bearing nor the appearance of Eliab for Samuel to think that he would be the chosen one of God. Yet God said that David would do everything He wanted him to do because David was a man after God's own heart (Acts 13:22).

Samuel's first instinct was to go with the tallest, most handsome man in the room, but God had a different choice, someone who was not even present. By all accounts, David was handsome, but he was merely a boy at the time of his anointing. With this story, God taught Samuel and us an important lesson: the way we look at the outward appearance of people can deceive us and lead us to make wrong judgments about them. If we ask God to open up our spiritual eyes to see what He sees, we will be able to make better decisions about our love lives.

How many times have you started relationships mainly because you are very physically attracted to the other person or because you have been dazzled by personality or professional success? "This is the one!" you might think. But God sees beyond that. He sees the essence of that person, the intentions of his heart, and his motivations. He also sees yours! When looking for a husband, it is very important to pray and ask God for direction and discernment to recognize that person, and not base your decision solely on what your eyes are seeing. Just because a person meets all your criteria, it doesn't necessarily mean that person is the one God has destined to be your husband. Your criteria might actually be wrong.

If I had chosen a husband based on the paradigms I had created, I wouldn't have married the amazing and loving husband that God blessed me with. Maybe I would still be single, waiting for my blessing. Or maybe I would have married the wrong person. Today, I know that God's perfect will for my life was Caleb, and it would have been impossible to recognize him as my husband if I had not fully surrendered my paradigms to God.

Many singles are being deceived. They have focused so much on their own convictions of what they want and have created such specific models in their minds about their future spouse that they forget to choose a partner following God's guidance. Their expectations and requirements often become the main obstacles to their finding love or to recognizing the man or woman God is putting before them. God doesn't follow any models or protocols when bringing two people together. With God, someone that is completely different from the spouse you have envisioned may be exactly what you have been looking for all your life. I encourage you to surrender to God all your paradigms about your future husband and allow Him to choose the right man for you.

CHAPTER 15

HONORING YOUR PARENTS

During the seven months that Caleb and I were friends, he asked me three times to be his girlfriend. The first two times, my answer was *no*. I didn't think he was the man God had destined to be my husband. But by the third time he asked, my thoughts about him had changed. I could now see him as more than just a friend. My response to Caleb was the following: "Any man who wants to have a relationship with me needs to first talk to the two most important men in my life. The first one is my dad, and the second one is my pastor." I didn't think Caleb would say *yes* to that. First of all, that required him traveling to my country. Second, there was the language barrier between Caleb and my family that would make communication difficult. Third, I didn't think he was that determined to have a relationship with me. To my surprise, he responded without hesitation, "I'm ready."

Long before I met Caleb, I had been praying to God for a confirmation about the man who would be my husband.

My prayer was: "Lord, may the man whom you have chosen to be my husband gain the trust, affection, and approval of my parents and my pastors. Let their hearts be at complete peace about him when they meet him."

It was time to know if this sign would be fulfilled. Talking to my parents and pastors was not going to be an easy feat for Caleb. My parents did not speak any English, and Caleb spoke very little Spanish. However, that was not an obstacle that stopped him. With a three-week intensive course of Spanish online and a plane ticket in hand, Caleb traveled to Mexico and had a man-to-man conversation first with my dad and days later, with my pastor.

Just as I asked in prayer, God confirmed with complete peace in the hearts of the people who love me the most that Caleb was a man who came from God's hand. Before having this confirmation, my parents, pastors, and I dedicated three weeks to pray about this matter. After which, God revealed that Caleb was the man who would be my husband. When I had no more doubts, I accepted his invitation to be his girlfriend. I knew that if I said *yes* to being his girlfriend, I was saying *yes* to becoming his wife as well. Two months after starting our relationship, we got engaged; and five months after the engagement, we were married.

My parent's opinion and approval on this matter were extremely important for me. Over the years, God had shown me that there is tremendous power and much blessing in *honoring my parents*. It is a lesson I learned the hard way though. I committed many mistakes and had great setbacks before I realized that when I disobeyed my parents or ignored their advice, I always had a lot of problems. But the opposite was also true. When I obeyed them and followed their advice, even when I didn't like it, there was great blessing and reward.

I have to be honest. When I was a teenager, I was rebellious, stubborn, and disobedient. I hated when my parents told me:

- "Do not do this."
- "Listen to me and obey. It's for your own good."
- "It would be best that you stop seeing that man. He is not a good person."

Normally, obeying our parents is not an easy thing. We want to do it our own way, not the way someone else is telling us to, right? However, when I was disobedient to my parents, the things they had warned me about inevitably happened. It didn't go well; in fact, it went pretty badly. My mother even said she had a "prophet's mouth" because everything that she said would happen if I did not follow her advice; it always came to pass.

I saw the following pattern repeating many times:

Obedience = blessing and reward.
Disobedience = problems, torment, and distress.

It was then that I decided to always seek the advice of my parents and follow it even if it was contrary to what I wanted to do. I even started to fear not following their advice or disobeying them, for I knew that I would severely limit any blessing I might receive from God if I disobeyed the authority placed over me by Him.

I started to practice obedience as a way of honoring not only my parents, but also God. The more I obeyed, the less difficult it became. Obedience became an act of resting and trusting in the direction that was given to me and letting God work on my behalf. Over and over again, God blessed my obedience because God honors those who honor Him, and you honor God when you honor and obey your parents.

(Note: There are instances in which parents are not around and cannot provide protection, guidance, and godly counsel to their children. I will talk more about this and what to do in this case in the second half of this chapter. There are also cases where parents are neglectful or abusive, and it is not God's plan for us to endure abuse at the hands of those who are meant to model Christ-like love. If you have been abused, or are being abused, seek help from a trusted, mature Christian leader in your life.)

A commandment with promise

> Children, obey your parents in the Lord, for this is right. "Honor your father and mother"—which is the first commandment with a promise—"so that it may go well with you and that you may enjoy long life on the earth." (Eph. 6:1–3, NIV)

The Bible says that honoring your father and your mother is the first commandment with a promise. What is the promise? That it may go well with you; God will bless you, prosper you, and make you succeed in everything you do.

God chose your parents and put them as authorities over you to guide you in the ways of life. God gave our parents an ability to see beyond what we see, perhaps because of the wisdom they have acquired over the years and because of the experiences that they have already lived.

"What do your parents say about the guy you are dating or are planning to date?" I asked this question to some of my single friends. The answers were varied:

- "I do not have a good relationship with my parents."
- "They do not know I am dating this person yet."
- "I do not live with them anymore. I haven't talked to them in a while."
- "I do not think they have any problems with my relationship."
- "They don't like him, but I really love him."
- "I do not know. I have not asked them yet."
- "I'm old enough to make my own decisions."
- "They know I am dating him. I think they like him."
- "They are okay with him."

These answers astonish me. Many single women today decide to start relationships without asking their parents' opinion and advice. Some choose not to follow the advice and end up doing what they think is best for them even if their parents disagree.

Including your parents in your decision to start a relationship with someone is not immature at all; it is actually a sign of spiritual maturity. It doesn't matter how old you are. For the record, I was twenty-nine and Caleb was thirty-four when he asked for my parents' permission to court me. Then he asked for their blessing before he proposed to me. It doesn't mean that you are not able to make your own decisions. Involving your parents is a matter of honor and of wanting to do things God's way.

A good friend once asked me "What if my boyfriend does not want to talk to my parents? I can't force him, can I?"

My response was, "No, you should not force him. But if this is important to you, then it should be important for him too. The man who really is into you, who wants to pursue you and has serious intentions about you, will have no problem talking to your parents."

The man who sees you as wife material should be more than excited to meet your parents and formally ask for their permission to date you and their blessing to marry you. Remember, you are the prize he wants to win! He should be willing to do whatever it takes to get you. If that is not the case, perhaps there is a problem, and you need to find out what that is. For example, maybe he is not committed to you, maybe he is not ready to formalize the relationship, maybe he is too shy, or maybe he doesn't like your parents. All these are warning signs that you must pay close attention to.

You decide the degree of formality or informality in your relationships; there are no protocols to follow. What is important is that you feel at peace and that your parents also agree on the decisions you are making about your love life. From my experience, however, when a man talks with your parents about his intentions toward you and his desire to date or marry you, it is a sign of formality, maturity, and commitment. It is a sign that he has no intention of wasting his time or yours. His goal is clear; he wants to start a relationship with the purpose of marrying you one day. This is a great demonstration of honor and respect to your parents that they will appreciate. As a result, you will feel secure, confident, cherished, honored, and respected as well. And let me tell you, that feeling is awesome!

Isaac, Rebekah, and the three confirmations

In the story of Isaac and Rebekah, we see the application of the principle of *honoring the parents*.

Abraham sent his servant to seek a wife for his son Isaac to the land where he had lived before. This was an important task for the servant; maybe he felt a bit nervous about the possibility of choosing the wrong woman or coming back empty-handed with no woman at all. This is why the servant asked Abraham the following:

> What if I can't find a young woman who is willing to go back with me? (Gen. 24:39, NLT)

Then Abraham responded:

> The Lord, in whose presence I have lived, will send his angel with you and will make your mission successful. Yes, you must find a wife for my son from among my relatives, from my father's family. Then you will have fulfilled your obligation. *But if you go to my relatives and they refuse to let her go with you, you will be free from my oath.* (Gen. 24:40–41, NLT)

Abraham had two requirements for the servant about the woman he would chose: she had to be a woman from his father's family, and the family of the young lady had to *consent* and *agree* to give their daughter as a wife to Isaac. This last one was a deal breaker for Abraham, for he knew the importance of *honoring the parents* of the woman.

As we learned in the chapter Divine Encounter, God prospered the journey of the servant when he found a beautiful young lady named Rebekah at a well. The Holy Spirit confirmed that she was the one he should choose when she gave him water and all of his camels. This was the sign the servant had prayed for and the first confirmation from God.

The servant asked Rebekah whose daughter she was and whether he could stay with her family. It turned out that Rebekah was the daughter of Abraham's relatives. This was the second confirmation.

> The young woman ran home to tell her family everything that had happened. (Gen. 24:28, NLT)

The attitude that Rebekah demonstrated showed that she had good communication with her family and meant that she looked for her parents' guidance. The servant went and met her parents, and told them all about his master Abraham, the journey he undertook to find a wife for Isaac, and how God confirmed with a signal that Rebekah was the woman he should chose. He then asked her parents' *permission* for Rebekah to go with him to become Isaac's wife.

Rebekah's parents' *consent* to let her go was the third confirmation from God (Gen. 24:50–51.) The parents also considered Rebekah's opinion and gave her a choice:

> Then they said, "Let's call the young woman and ask her about it." So they called Rebekah and asked her, "Will you go with this man?"
> "I will go," she said. (Gen. 24:57–58, NIV)

God confirmed three times that Rebekah was going to be Isaac's wife. Notice that Rebekah's parents did not give their consent based on their own opinion, for they said, "This is totally from God. We have no say in the matter, either yes or no." (Gen. 24:50, MSG). Rebekah's parents were people that feared the Lord and were in tune with the Spirit of God. Under ordinary circumstances, it would have been negligent to let their daughter go with a stranger. But this was not an ordinary situation, for God's intervention in this encounter had been manifested through various signs and confirmations. The Lord made it very clear to all that this was His plan.

The marriage of Isaac and Rebekah was, from beginning to end, a decision of faith guided by the Holy Spirit. *Abraham had faith* that God would send his angel before the servant to prosper his journey. *The servant had faith* in asking for a sign of confirmation from God when he saw the woman at the well. *Rebekah's parents had faith* that God had planned it all. *Rebekah had faith* that Isaac was the man God had destined to be her future husband even before she met him. *Isaac had faith* that Rebekah was the woman God had destined to be his wife from the first time he saw her.

Faith is the ultimate element needed to receive a husband or wife from God. When you are looking for your husband, it is important that your decisions are based on faith. This should include putting God first, seeking the guidance of the Holy Spirit, and considering the counsel and guidance of your parents.

There are a few things to highlight about this love story. First, God does everything in order. Second, He confirms when two people are meant to be husband and wife. Third, the principle of *honoring your parents* is part of God's order and should not be ignored when looking for a spouse.

Whether you are planning to start dating someone or planning to get married, it is extremely important to allow your parents be involved in these important decisions. When you honor your parents, you honor God. He will bless you and reward you because you are doing things His way.

The difference between worldly dating and courtship

The story of Isaac and Rebekah is not only a great example that applies to the principle of *honoring the parents*; it is also the biblical model of what a romantic relationship between a single man and a single woman can be like. In this story, there is no reference to a time of *dating*, for the Bible says that when Isaac saw Rebekah for the first time, he brought her into the tent of his mother Sarah and married her (Gen. 24:67).

The concept of *dating* in the Bible does not exist. *Dating* is a modern approach to finding love. Dating comes in different forms. Some people date in a *friendship* way for a long time before starting a formal relationship or getting engaged. Others date *romantically* from the moment they meet. Sometimes they end up married, and sometimes they don't. Some people have sexual intimacy when they are dating while others decide to abstain until they get married.

Perhaps for many couples, *dating* has been a fine approach to finding love and getting married. Nevertheless, I believe that for every *dating* success story, there are hundreds or even thousands of stories of heartbreak, pain, disappointment, frustration, confusion, and time wasted. Why? Because in the majority of cases, *dating* lacks commitment and guidance from the Holy Spirit.

There are two approaches to dating: *worldly dating* and *godly dating* (also called *courtship*). Let's examine the difference between the two.

Worldly dating is highly influenced by the world's system:

- It is *casual*; relationships can be as short as just a few days or as long as several years.
- It often *lacks commitment*; it normally does not initiate with marriage as the goal of the relationship.
- The choice of a partner is primarily *based on physical attraction and chemistry*.
- This model *is selfish*; it pursues instant sexual, physical, and emotional gratification with no ties or assumed responsibilities.
- Relationships are highly *susceptible to sexual sin (premarital sex)*.
- It *is loose*; it is easy to walk into a relationship and to quickly end it if it is not convenient.

In a nutshell, *worldly dating* can be extremely messy, resulting in much suffering, sorrow, heartbreak and wasted time. For me, dating was always a dead-end; it led nowhere. It only left my heart broken and wounded. I believe that *worldly dating* was never God's plan for love relationships for He is a God of covenant.

A better option for the worldly idea of dating is *courtship*. The concept of courtship is not in the Bible either; however, it is a more godly approach to finding love.

Courtship is highly influenced by God's standards:

- It is a *short to medium-term dating relationship* that begins with the goal of marriage.
- In courtship, both *people are committed* from the beginning.
- There is normally *prayerful consideration* before starting the relationship.
- It is a *decision of faith*.

- People *abstain from sex* until marriage.
- People *honor their parents* by seeking their opinion, approval, and blessings throughout the process.

The following table summarizes the differences between *worldly dating* and *courtship*:

Love on Hold Worldly Dating Vs. Courtship Comparison Table	
Worldly Dating	Courtship
Relationship based primarily on sexual and physical attraction. The spiritual aspect is not a priority.	Relationship based primarily on the spiritual aspect. Physical attraction is important but is not the priority.
It normally does not start with the purpose of marriage in the near future.	Starts with a single purpose: marriage in the near future.
It can become a long-term relationship (lasting several years) with or without marriage plans in the future.	It is generally a short-term relationship that can last a couple of months to a year prior to getting married.
It is a generally casual relationship that lacks commitment.	It is a formal relationship with commitment.
God is not necessarily considered in the process of looking for a partner.	Seeking God's guidance is extremely important during the process of looking for a partner. The relationship starts when there is conviction or confirmation that God is uniting the two people (e.g. Isaac and Rebekah).

The relationship, if conducted in a worldly fashion, has a high chance of rupture. If it comes to an end, both people are emotionally affected.	There is less chance of rupture when both parties are committed to a godly process leading to marriage.
Parents may not be taken into account.	Parents play a major role giving direction, counsel, approval, and blessing.
It may not build a strong foundation for marriage.	It builds a foundation for marriage success, teaching principles of self-control and waiting for God's timing.
It can be based on the *eros* love (love that comes from physical attraction, sexual gratification, lust, passion, and sexual desire.) It seeks personal satisfaction over the satisfaction of the other person.	It is based on the *agape* love (the one that comes from God. It is a love that is sacrificial and unconditional). Its priority is the satisfaction and well-being of the other person over self-satisfaction.

For me, dating was just a waste of time and an emotional roll-ercoaster that caused much pain. When I finally got tired of it, I decided to do things God's way. (If only I would have done it this way from the beginning!) I decided to abstain from dating and to wait for the man who was ready to have a courtship relationship with me. I recommend that you consider doing the same. It might keep you from wasting valuable time and help you avoid many dis-appointments and heartbreaks.

Spend most of your time knowing the other person as a friend. *Friendship* is a relationship where there is no kissing, caressing, flirting, talking about the future as a couple, insinuating some-thing more than a friendship or anything of the like. If after being friends for a while, you and the other person think that you are destined to be husband and wife, then that's the right time to start a courtship. Remember, courtship is a preparation time before marriage, and it should be short. A couple of months to a year would be best, but time length may vary from couple to couple. Long-term courtships can lead to sexual temptation and sin; thus, they are not ideal.

Friendship is the best foundation for a successful marriage. Sadly, most people skip this important stage and begin a romantic relationship almost immediately because they are physically attracted to each other. Often times, the result is a relationship lacking a solid foundation. Most importantly, don't forget to seek your parent's guidance, wisdom, and counsel when you start a courting relationship.

What if your parents are not around?

There might be instances in which biological parents are not there for their children due to death, abandonment, abuse, being unbelievers, or other circumstances. In such cases, who can provide guidance to the single woman? If this is your case, you can seek the direction, wisdom, and advice of another Christian believer. It can be a relative such as your grandparents, an uncle, or older sibling, for example. It can also be your pastor, a church leader, or another person God has placed in your life to be your spiritual mentor or spiritual mother or father.

A spiritual mentor is a person that:

- is under the lordship of Christ,
- has spiritual wisdom,
- knows you, loves you, and is genuinely interested in your well-being,
- has accepted to provide spiritual protection for you,
- is willing and available to give you advice, instruction, correction, and direction when you need it,
- you can trust and respect.

If you need a spiritual mentor, ask God who that person could be. Once He reveals that to you, go to that person and ask them if they can mentor you. If they accept, then you can start looking for their guidance, advice, and prayer; but you must also accept their correction. Remember, that person will become like a spiritual parent to you, so you should submit to their wisdom.

If you are attending a church in which you have no relationship with your pastors or leaders and they do not even know your name, it may be because you have not introduced yourself to them yet. I encourage you to go, introduce yourself, share a little, and start looking for someone you can be accountable to and who can help you. If you feel that in your church you cannot find someone who genuinely cares about you or can help you, it might be a good idea to look for another church.

The widow, the divorced, and the single mother

The Bible says that for the widowed and the abandoned, the Lord Almighty is her husband (Isa. 54:4–5, NIV). She who has been left alone should put her hope in God and pray continuously, asking Him for help (1 Tim. 5:5, NIV). While Isaiah 54:4–5 is speaking to the children of Israel after they came out of captivity, the literal words to the widowed and abandoned ring true: the Lord Almighty is her husband. If you are a widow, divorced, abandoned, or single mother, God is your husband; but it is up to you to seek Him diligently in prayer for direction.

However, it is also important to have a physical person from whom you can receive counsel, direction, and advice. You can always look for the counsel of your parents or find refuge under the protection and care of a spiritual mentor.

Women of the Bible mentored by people other than their parents

The Bible gives several examples of women whose biological parents were not there for them but who found protection and wisdom in the form of another person. Let's look at some of them:

Esther

> Mordecai had a cousin named Hadassah,
> whom he had brought up because she had nei-
> ther father nor mother. This young woman, who
> was also known as Esther, had a lovely figure
> and was beautiful. Mordecai had taken her as his
> own daughter when her father and mother died.
> (Esther 2:7, NIV)

Esther's father and mother died, and she was raised under the care of another person, her cousin Mordecai. Esther honored and obeyed Mordecai as if he was her father. She sought his advice and was obedient to it.

Esther honored, respected, and obeyed Mordecai in everything. The result of Esther walking under his care and direction was the blessing of God over her life. Not only did she become queen when King Xerxes chose her to be his wife, but she also achieved the purpose of God: to bring salvation and deliverance for all the Jews who were her people.

Ruth

Ruth was a young widow who sought the care and direction of her mother-in-law Naomi. Ruth clung to Naomi as if she were her own mother.

Naomi was a woman who was devoted to God, full of wisdom, and who loved Ruth as a daughter. Ruth knew she needed someone to watch over her and could provide godly counsel to her. Naomi became for Ruth a spiritual mother and mentor.

Throughout the story of Ruth, there are numerous times when Naomi advises Ruth what to say and what to do in certain circumstances. Ruth honored Naomi not only by taking care of her but also by being obedient to her instruction. Since Ruth honored Naomi, God honored Ruth by blessing her with a godly husband, Boaz.

All of us as women need to have a Naomi in our lives. Naomi is a spiritual mentor, a woman who can be your mother, or another woman who loves you and cares for you as a mother and who has godly wisdom to give you good advice and correct you.

Seek and follow

I would like to close this chapter by encouraging you to seek and follow the advice of your parents, or whoever your spiritual mentor is. I know that this concept of walking under your parents' guidance and authority may be difficult to understand if you have grown up as an independent woman and you have learned over the years not to consult anyone and to always make your own decisions. I understand your way of thinking because I was also in that situation, and it was difficult at first to seek advice and direction. However, as I began to walk under the authority that God had placed over my life, being obedient to the parental and other godly direction I was given, God opened doors of blessing into my life. That is the wisdom that I want to share with you. That when you honor the authority God has established over you, He honors and blesses you.

As a single woman, look for the direction and advice of your parents in your journey to find love. I say this to you as a woman who experienced both sides of the coin: doing things my way and getting hurt by men who were not worth it, and doing things God's way. When I followed the direction of my parents, I experienced the most beautiful courtship and marriage I could have ever imagined.

If your parents are not part of your life or are not able to provide the godly counsel and direction that you need, think about who might be the best person to become your spiritual mentor. Ask for help and direction from the Holy Spirit so that he will reveal to you who that person might be. Once you encounter that person, hold fast to the counsel and instruction they are going to give you because *honoring* is key to attaining the blessings of God.

CHAPTER 16

A MUTUAL COMMITMENT TO PURITY

After getting the blessing and permission from my parents and pastors, Caleb and I started a courtship. We both knew that the purpose of the relationship was to get married in a short amount of time. For the first time, my heart was at peace in the arms of a man who was completely committed to our relationship. Since we lived in different places, we traveled to see each other regularly. When I traveled to see Caleb, I stayed at a friend's house; when he traveled to see me, he stayed in a hotel. We decided to stay in separate places to avoid being alone in private and falling into sexual temptation. From the beginning, we had the conviction of keeping our relationship pure even though we had not talked about what our physical boundaries would be.

As we started kissing, I began to wonder what kind of boundaries I should establish to keep the relationship within God's standards. "How much is too much? What kind of physical touch is allowed that does not compromise our faith? At what point does a caress become sin?" I wondered. "Should I wait until something inappropriate is about to happen to have a conversation with Caleb?" All these questions began to spin in my head. The same questions and concerns were also in Caleb's mind, though I did not know it.

We wanted to do things right, honoring God with our bodies and respecting each other. We didn't want to do anything that was inappropriate or sinful. But how could we stand firm in our convictions of faith and not yield to the seduction of physical and sexual temptation? It would be something hard to accomplish unless we made a mutual commitment to purity. That's when we had "the talk."

The gift box

Caleb and I were at a cafeteria in the Austin airport, waiting for my flight to Monterrey. I had traveled that weekend to spend time with him. We were talking and having fun when Caleb said to me, "Cintia, I want to ask you a question. I need to know your thoughts."

"Sure, what's going on?" I answered.

"I want to know what is allowed and what is not allowed regarding our physical treatment? I want you to feel comfortable at all times, and I want to respect you and honor God."

I smiled. I thought he was a real gentleman and godly man by asking me a question like that. But I did not know exactly what to answer. Then I said, "Umm, well obviously, sex is not allowed. Nor any caresses that take us too far and make us fall into sexual temptation."

Caleb nodded in agreement.

"Okay, look. Let's do something," he answered. Then he took a napkin and a pen, and started to draw something on it while I observed in silence what he was doing. "What is this?" He asked, showing me his drawing.

"Umm, it looks like a soccer field," I said.

"Yeah! It's a soccer field!" he said. "We are the players in a game. Everything that is within the field, we are allowed to do; but everything outside the field, we are not allowed to do. So let's start writing those things that are allowed inside the field and those that are not allowed outside of it."

I just rolled my eyes, smiled, and thought, *Soccer field? He is such a boy!* Then I said, "I have a better idea. Instead of a soccer field, let's pretend that this square is a gift box. Everything we write inside the gift box is reserved for marriage. Everything we write outside the box, we can enjoy it during courtship. The gift box will be our wedding gift, and we can open it once we are married."

"Oh! That sounds even better!" he exclaimed, and we both started laughing.

Before writing something inside or outside the box, we first asked each other, "What do you think about this?" and as we came to an agreement, we wrote it on paper. It was a fairly easy exercise, and it was easy to distinguish what should go inside and what should go outside the box. As we did it, we were being accountable to each other with what we were agreeing to. This exercise allowed us to draw the line of what was acceptable and permissible in terms of physical treatment according to our faith.

Once Caleb and I finished writing, we prayed that God would witness our mutual commitment to purity. This exercise was extremely helpful. It helped us to stand firm and resist sexual temptation. By writing it on paper, it had also been written in our minds, our spirits, and our hearts.

Things left outside the box:

- kisses on the lips, face, hands, arms, and neck,
- hugs,
- holding hands.

Things left inside the box:

- lying down together,
- having sex,
- taking off our clothes,
- touching genital areas and breasts,
- caresses under the clothes,
- kisses in places other than the ones allowed.

I think this talk is something every Christian couple should have at the beginning of a relationship. Because if you don't have it, you are not accountable to each other, and you might not be on the same page with the other person regarding what is allowed and what is not. It can be very easy to fall into sexual temptation. It is also very likely that along the way, there are misunderstandings and different expectations that can cause problems.

For example, if your boyfriend wants to touch you in a way that you feel compromises the purity of the relationship, he may feel rejected and embarrassed the moment you stop him. He might think, "Maybe she does not like me touching her," or "Maybe she is not attracted to me." On the other hand, he may not touch you or kiss you in a way you would like because he doesn't want you to feel uncomfortable by him going too far. You might think, "Maybe he does not find me attractive enough," or "He does not love me." My advice is that from the beginning, both of you talk about what is acceptable and permissible instead of waiting until it is too late.

Waiting to have that conversation until both of you are in the midst of a moment of passion can cause the moment to become quite awkward. You might not even be able to stop, and you will end up going further than you would have wanted.

Emotional stability will come with moral purity

Pam and Chris met on a dating website. Each of them had been married before, and both had gone through a divorce. They wanted another chance to find love and marry again if God allowed them to meet someone special. Fortunately, from the first day they met in person, they hit it off. They had so much fun together, they were equally passionate about their faith, and they also were very attracted to each other.

They started to hang out as friends, and within a few dates, Chris tried to kiss Pam. As much as Pam wanted that kiss, she stopped him and said, "I have been single seven years and I haven't kissed anybody. The last person I kissed was my ex-husband, and the next person I will kiss will be my new husband." Chris was pleasantly surprised about her statement. Pam's conviction to guard her heart and body for her future husband made her more desirable and interesting in Chris's eyes. He immediately felt more respect and appreciation for her and wanted to kiss her even more! But that night, he had to wait. Long story short, they got married a few months later, and their first kiss was at their wedding.

Today, Pam says, "I didn't kiss Chris before marrying him because I wanted both of us to know each other without adding all of that physical stuff into our relationship. Once you start kissing and touching each other, the focus of the relationship changes. You don't think as objectively anymore because now, there are a lot of emotions and physical stimuli in the mix. It really distracts you from knowing the other person for who they are. So that's why we waited, and it was so worth it!"

———— ♡♡ ————

Pam knew the importance and power of abstaining from physical intimacy while dating. Abstinence, rather than taking away something from the relationship, actually adds a lot of good things to it. It adds respect, honor, trust, commitment, desire, expectation, excitement, and most importantly, a love that is pure and unselfish.

Something I was able to realize by keeping my relationship with Caleb pure was that I enjoyed mental clarity and emotional stability all the time. This was really awesome! I never felt insecure, needy, or more invested in the relationship than he did. Our commitment to purity allowed us to know each other deeply and intimately without having to touch our bodies inappropriately, and thus compromise our faith. We experienced complete fulfillment in our relationship and a unique kind of love and joy that we had never experienced before.

Sexual and physical intimacy before marriage can cloud your thinking and emotions. Many women lose the ability to think objectively and make the right decisions after they have been touched intimately or had sex with a man. When a man touches a woman's body or has sex with her, he also touches her soul. For a woman, it is impossible to have sex without her emotions being touched. Once her soul is touched, she stops thinking objectively and starts making decisions based on feelings and emotions that may be misleading.

Our Heavenly Father wants us to guard our heart and to give it only to the man who will cherish it and will take care of it—our husband.

> Guard your heart above all else, for it determines the course of your life. (Prov. 4:23, NLT)

What does it mean *to guard* our heart and how can we do this? *To guard* means: to protect, to take care of something, to put something in a place so that it is not lost or altered, to keep something in good condition. It also means to "keep confined or to protect [as something precious]."[19] You can guard your heart by not doing what is wrong, impure, immoral, or unpleasant in God's eyes. One effective way to guard your heart is by not having physical intimacy outside of marriage.

The consequences of playing with fire

"How far can I get physically with my partner without committing sin?" This is the question that plagues the minds of many believers. This is similar to asking, "How much can I play with fire without burning myself?" It is not a matter of how far you can get physically with your partner without committing sin, but about avoiding any situation that could potentially lead to it. Inevitably, the one who plays with fire will end up getting burned, just as the one who plays with physical intimacy will end up sinning.

— ♡ —

Roxanne was very excited when she started dating Jorge. He was attentive, affectionate, and formal; he treated her like a princess. Roxanne felt loved and cherished. They agreed early on not to have sex until marriage. Although neither of them were virgins, and they

---

[19] Richards, Lawrence O. *New International Encyclopedia of Bible Words* (Grand Rapids, MI: Zondervan, 1991), p. 322

both knew it, they had decided that in their relationship, they would honor God with their bodies.

As time went by and the relationship developed, they felt closer than ever. Roxanne was confident that Jorge would be her husband, and she thought that it was only a matter of time until he proposed. One day, while they were alone, the kisses and caresses between them went a little further than usual. They began to touch and kiss each other in places that made them feel aroused and created sexual tension. That day, neither of them said anything at all; they just decided to enjoy the moment. Roxanne thought that as long as there was no intercourse, everything would be fine. However, as time went on, these intimate moments continued to escalate. The relationship became more physical than Roxanne would have wanted, but she didn't say anything because she feared looking old-fashioned or boring to Jorge. She continued to allow his moves.

The relationship began to get empty and cold. Roxanne started to feel very insecure. Intrusive thoughts and doubts tormented her. "Does Jorge really love me? I wonder if our physical intimacy has changed the way he feels about me." Finally, overwhelmed by feelings of fear and guilt, Roxanne spoke with Jorge and voiced her concerns about the physicality of their relationship. After listening to her, Jorge told her that there was nothing wrong with what they had done. After all, they had not had intercourse. Roxanne sighed with relief for a moment, but in her heart, she continued to feel a lack of peace.

Roxanne was deeply distressed and more confused than ever. These emotions clouded her ability to think and decide objectively. She wanted to continue to please Jorge and enjoy those moments of intimacy with him; however, those moments of momentary pleasure brought a deep and constant feeling of guilt and remorse within her. She knew that what they were doing was sin. One day, the physical treatment between them went too far. In a moment of passion, the sexual tension reached such a point that they could not stop, and they had sex.

The next day, they both were convinced that what had happened the night before was wrong. Far from feeling closer to each other, they felt embarrassed, regretful, and distant. They decided to ask each other for forgiveness and to ask Gods' forgiveness as well. They thought that from then on, everything would be back to normal. However, the relationship between them never went back to what it was at first: exciting, fun, spontaneous, and joyful. Something had been permanently turned off, corrupted, and damaged.

Jorge became more distant than ever; Roxanne became more insecure and in need of affirmation as time went by. Sadly, the relationship only lasted a few more months and ended, leaving both of them deeply hurt.

Roxanne stated the following, "I know that if Jorge and I had kept the relationship pure, the story would have been very different. Maybe we would be engaged and planning our wedding right now. The relationship was beautiful and perfect when our physical treatment was pure. Everything began to change from the moment we began to touch and kiss in inappropriate ways—ways that we both knew were unpleasant to God. Sin infiltrated, and little by little, it ruined all things. If only I could go back and do things differently. Unfortunately, that is no longer possible."

Roxanne is still a single woman. Her deepest desire is to find a man that has the same convictions of purity that she now has. She is confident that her next relationship will be very different from the previous one. Physical boundaries will be set from the beginning. She has decided to completely abstain from sexual intimacy and to guard her body from now until marriage.

Love does not dishonor others

> It (love) does not dishonor others, it is not self-seeking." (1 Cor. 13:5, NIV)

Do not be deceived by the false belief that in order to prove your love to your partner, you must have sex before marriage. The

Bible says in 1 Corinthians 13:4–7 that love takes no pleasure in evil, it does not dishonor others, and it is not self-seeking. It does not put pressure or manipulation on the other person to get what it wants. On the contrary, love is patient and is kind, it rejoices in the truth and in doing what is right before God. Love is pure and kind; it endures everything. That is the proof of true love.

Having sex before marriage is not *love* but *lust* of the flesh. The best way to not fall into sexual temptation is by having an early, open communication with your partner about what will be the physical boundaries of the relationship. The gift box and the soccer field are examples of practical and easy ways to achieve a mutual commitment to purity. Simply writing the boundaries down together on paper establishes a foundation of good communication and respect between you and the person who will possibly become your husband someday.

Having good communication about what is acceptable and what is not is something that you and your future husband will need for the rest of your lives. You will need this same type of conversation about finances or how to raise your children. Setting physical boundaries in the relationship might be challenging, but it comes with great reward. The reward is a foundation of true love, mutual respect, patience, and honor to God.

In addition, having "the talk" will make you responsible and accountable to each other for your actions. It will help you walk together in the same direction. Believe me, there are going to be times when you will want to break the rules and cross the boundaries, and your partner will remind you of the commitment you both made. Or maybe he is going to be the one who wants to cross the boundaries, and you will be able remind him of the commitment you both made before God at the beginning of the relationship. The responsibility is mutual. If you both do not walk hand in hand toward the same goal, sooner or later, you will stumble and fall.

Satan is your adversary. He will try everything to seduce you and make you fall into temptation. Perhaps God has a great purpose for you and the person you are dating. Perhaps His plan is for you both to form a godly marriage in Christ, but Satan is going to present temptations to destroy God's plan. What could have been a beautiful relationship established on a foundation of purity will be damaged and corrupted by sin.

> Though one may be overpowered, two can defend themselves. A *cord of three strands* is not quickly broken. (Eccles. 4:12, NIV)

Perhaps you alone might not be able to flee from sexual immorality when it is presented, but the Bible says that two can withstand the enemy better than one. There is power in unity! If you and your partner have made a commitment before God, it will be easier for you to stand firm and not fall into temptation. Your relationship will be like that *cord of three strands* the Bible talks about that is not quickly broken. You and your partner are the first two strands, joined and strengthened by a third and even more powerful one, the Holy Spirit.

Here are five practical steps you can follow to keep your relationship pure:

1. *Talk.* Have a conversation with your partner about the physical limits as early as possible.
2. *Commit.* Reach a mutual agreement about what is permissible and what is not and commit to it. If possible, write it on paper so that both of you are witnesses to what you have agreed on and are able to remember in the future (e.g. the gift box or the soccer field).
3. *Avoid.* Avoid being alone in places that can present an opportunity to have physical intimacy beyond the limits that you have established. Avoid lying down together anywhere.
4. *Revisit.* If there is something that bothers you and that you feel is compromising the purity of the relationship, don't be afraid or embarrassed to talk to your partner as soon as possible. Revisit the boundaries of purity with them and come to an agreement again.

5. *Repent.* If there is anything that you have to repent of, do it together before God and renew your commitment of purity.

It is never too late to straighten the path and turn away from evil. It will require a lot of faith, self-denial, and determination, but it is possible.

Save your body and heart for the man who will be your husband and for that special moment of your wedding night. The gift box will add a tremendous level of excitement and expectation to your honeymoon. It will be beautiful to finally open it after working so hard to keep it untouched. Best of all, there will be no fear, guilt, remorse, shame, or anything to hide. The intimacy between you and your husband will be pure, holy, and blessed, just as God designed it to be.

CHAPTER 17

IT WAS WORTH THE WAIT!

It was an April afternoon. The moment I had waited for all my life had finally arrived, the day of my wedding. My hair and makeup were done, I had my dress and veil on; I was ready. I looked through the window of the room and saw the beautiful hacienda garden where in a few hours, the religious ceremony would take place. There in the silence and solitude of that moment, I began to remember my journey as a single woman.

I meditated on many moments and situations I encountered during my previous twenty-nine years. Thinking about the times I felt sad and lonely, when I was heartbroken and suffered major relationship disappointments, I just smiled. I knew that I would not keep those memories anymore. Those things had such an emotional weight in the past, but now were so irrelevant. Little by little, they would fade until they would exist no more. Then I thought about the good times. When thinking about the moments with my family and friends and the many meaningful relationships I made, I breathed a long, nostalgic sigh. I knew those would be people and memories I would never forget, and time would never take those away.

Among mixed emotions, God was preparing my heart for embracing the next season of my life as a married woman. I would leave my home, family, friends, and country forever to start a new journey with Caleb, the love of my life, the man God had destined to be my husband.

Then the Holy Spirit brought to my remembrance the day when I surrendered to God that love relationship with the man from Canada. "Cintia, do you remember the promise I gave you when you laid down your dream at My feet?" I nodded. Of course, I remembered! I fixed my eyes to the sky as the Holy Spirit recited God's words in my heart:

> My daughter, I have plans of good for you. If you surrender your dreams to Me, I will open up doors of opportunity and a path for you where there is none. I will fulfill the deepest desires and longings of your heart. One day, you will be ready to go, and you will know when the time will come because I will reveal it to you. And I will go with you, and I will bless you, because you put your trust in Me.

As His words overflowed in my spirit, I marveled at God's faithfulness, His might, and His unique ways of fulfilling His promises. It was not too late, not too early, but perfectly right on time. When God gives a promise, He never fails to make it come to pass. God does everything beautifully in His time.

While I meditated on all this, God showed me that every moment I had lived, both good and bad, were like pieces of a puzzle that when put together, form our destiny. All the moments of my life, even the most painful disappointments and breakups, had been necessary for me to become the woman that I was, the one Caleb had fallen in love with. All those moments were strangely but divinely interconnected with each other and had built the path that took me right there, to the day in which I would say *I do* to my future husband.

The wedding night

That day, Caleb and I had decided we would not see each other until I walked down the aisle. The time came when the religious ceremony started. Caleb walked down the aisle accompanied by his parents and then the orchestra began to play the "Wedding March." All the guests prepared to receive the bride. Finally, I came out and walked on that red carpet in my white dress. I felt excited, happy, and expectant about what the future had in store for us. As I walked down the aisle, I could see him in the distance, patiently waiting for me at the altar. When he saw me for the first time, his eyes filled with tears of happiness. I could not help but laugh for joy, thinking, *There he is, my future husband, my blessing, the promise of God fulfilled!*

I got to where he was. We took each other's hands and smiled nervously. For a moment, we lost ourselves in our gazes. Without saying any words, we knew exactly what we were thinking. We were amazed at the faithfulness of God, at how He had united us in supernatural and unexpected ways. Our journeys as singles in waiting had been long and sometimes difficult, but that day, they had come to an end. The mercy of God had reached us. At last, our eyes could see the answer to our persistent prayers for a spouse.

At the end of the ceremony, we proceeded to have a reception with the guests in the grand salon of the Hotel Quinta Real. Caleb and I danced our first song together, "When God Made You" by NewSong. It's one of the most beautiful love songs I've ever heard. Each line of that song really reflected our feelings for each other and our story as a man and woman waiting to receive the miracle of love. During the waiting time, when there were so many questions without answers, there was God, preparing the moment of our divine encounter. I have no doubt that as the song says, *"The day God made my husband, He must have been thinking about me."* Because in Caleb, I found everything I needed and more than I had ever dreamed of.

Songs of praise and adoration set the scene throughout the night. By midnight, the wedding was over. There were still some guests dancing when Caleb and I said our goodbyes and let the people continue to enjoy the music. We retired to our hotel room where we would spend the first night together.

When we got to our bedroom, there was an iced bottle of champagne and a plate of chocolate-covered strawberries waiting for us, a courtesy of the hotel. Caleb and I got comfortable and sat on the couch. We made a toast to our marriage, our first night together, and our future. We did not stop laughing; we felt an indescribable joy that we could not contain. My soul was in complete peace and rest at Caleb's side. Never before had I experienced that kind of fulfillment in the arms of a man.

We were both a little nervous, but it was a good feeling. We had been waiting for that much-anticipated time alone as a married couple. For the first time, we were together as husband and wife.

We noticed that on the bed, there was a *gift box*. We got closer and saw there was a card with the following inscription:

My beloved children,

It has pleased Me to unite your lives today and forever. A great adventure is ahead of you; I will be with you always. For now, rejoice and enjoy my wedding gift. Enter into the joy of your Lord.

Your Heavenly Father

Caleb and I embraced each other. The gift box that we had saved for so long, and had been careful not to disturb, was finally ready to be opened and enjoyed.

Caleb pulled one end of the white ribbon that adorned the box, and I pulled the other. Then we proceeded to remove the wrap and carefully took away the lid. There, at the bottom of the box, was what we had long waited for, what we had taken care not to corrupt: *pure and sublime intimacy.* The presence of God filled our room, and we delighted in the gift that our Heavenly Father had given us.

The journey to reach that point had been long, but the anguish of waiting did not compare with the glory and beauty of obtaining the promise. Once again, I could witness that God makes everything beautiful and perfect in His time. That night, I laid down in peace, with joy of heart, embraced by the arms of my now beloved husband.

I closed my eyes, sighed deeply, and as I prepared to sleep, my heart whispered, "Thank you very much, Lord. It was worth the wait."

Right on track

From the moment God promised me He would bless me with a husband until the moment I saw this promise fulfilled, it was exactly seven years. During those years, I thought I was ready to receive that blessing, but I was not. Those years were, in fact, necessary; God used them to prepare me for marriage.

As a single woman, I committed a lot of mistakes. Many times, I did things without seeking God's direction. I was rebellious when I did not listen to the advice and counsel of my parents, I made wrong decisions, I fell into temptations, and of course, there were various men who broke my heart. If I received God's blessing, it was not because I had done things perfectly but because He is merciful.

I reached a point where I got tired of suffering and wasting my time dating guys that were not serious or ready for commitment. My way of doing things was not working. I knew that while I was in control of my love life, I would not get anywhere. When I finally surrendered completely my desire for love to God and gave Him control of everything, that's when He began to straighten things out and open the way for me to receive the blessing of a husband, a man after God's own heart.

While I was waiting all those years, I could not understand what God was doing or why the fulfillment of the promise seemed to take so long. Many times, I felt overwhelmed by emotions of sadness, loneliness, and discouragement. I dared to ask God, "Why, Lord, do you not answer me? Why do you take so long to bless me?" However, today, I can finally understand that every day and year I waited was not a *delay* but rather the *journey* toward my blessing, the path I needed to walk.

Everything you have experienced, including the moment in which you are right now, is the *journey* to your promise. The journey is full of mountains and valleys. One day, you will feel at the top of the mountain; other days, you will feel at the bottom of a valley.

But both of these are part of the journey that day by day prepares you, strengthens your faith, shapes your character, and leads you to depend more on God. Your story is not over yet, God keeps writing it. Follow the journey with your eyes fixed on Christ, and you will arrive at your destination.

One day, your eyes will be able to see the love promise you have been praying for. When that day comes, you will smile and with a joyful heart will say, "It was worth the wait."

CHAPTER 18

FINAL EXHORTATIONS

What inspired me to write this book was you, my dear single friend. I know your longing for love. I can relate to that feeling of loneliness that sometimes afflicts you. I fought the battles that you are facing as a single woman; and I know the doubts, fears, and insecurities that have sometimes assaulted you. God allowed me to live my own journey in order to be able to speak to your heart, to comfort you, to encourage you, and to give you hope.

As you can see, you are not alone in this journey to find love. Most single women start their quest for the love of a man from a very young age, perhaps too young to be ready for it. God has placed that longing for love in our hearts, and it is His desire and perfect will to fulfill it.

As you have almost finished reading this book, there are three things I would like you to take away and to always remember:

- *Make God's word your standard*

> The grass withers and the flowers fade, but
> the word of our God stands forever. (Isa. 40:8)

Your story and journey as a single woman is unique; very different from mine or from any other's journey. I'm sure you have had experiences that I've never lived and struggles that I never encountered. Quite possibly, our age is not the same and neither are our roots and upbringings. Despite our journeys being so different, there is something that is universal, that does not change, and that applies to any situation for generations and generations: the Word of God.

All the principles you have learned in this book are based on the Bible. If you follow the instruction that God has given us in His Word and you seek the direction of the Holy Spirit, I guarantee you will succeed in everything that you set your mind and heart to, including finding love. Follow the Word of God, make it your guide and standard of living, and it will go well with you.

- *Do not be shaped by this world*

> Don't copy the behavior and customs of this world, but let God transform you into a new person by changing the way you think. Then you will learn to know God's will for you, which is good and pleasing and perfect. (Rom. 12:2, NLT)

This is not a book about a new model of finding love, but it is about the original model that God designed from the beginning. A model where there is commitment, purity, honor, and intervention of the Holy Spirit.

God's model and the world's model to find a partner contradict each other. As you already learned in this book, the model of the world offers relationships without commitment based merely on physical attraction. It also encourages sex and physical intimacy before marriage. The world also suggests dressing provocatively to get the attention of men, initiating relationships with married men, spending the night with your boyfriend, etc. All of this is out of God's order and God's will, and none of this will lead you to find true love.

Do not let the world be your standard for finding love. God has a higher and excellent calling for you, which does not compare to anything this world has to offer. Therefore, do not settle, do not copy the world and its patterns, do not give up. Strive to be the woman that God has called you to be, a woman of faith, set apart from sexual immorality and sin. It is worth surrendering your desire for love to God and waiting for Him to bring the blessing of a husband to your life. It is worth abstaining from having sex and physical intimacy before marriage and saving your body for the man who will be your husband.

You are very loved and precious to God. You are His daughter, His chosen one, God's special possession (1 Pet. 2:9). So do not let any man make fun of you or despise you because of your faith, beliefs, and standards. Do not let a man who wants a relationship without commitment or who disrespects you physically or verbally into your life. Because that man does not come from God, and he will only hurt you and waste your precious time.

Listen to me well. There is a man out there that God is preparing for you, a man who is looking for a wife, who might be praying and is waiting for the blessing of knowing you. When God introduces you to that man, he will be able to recognize you as the woman he has been looking and waiting for. He will be ready and more than willing to fight for you. That man knows that you are worth the wait, just as you've been waiting for him. So do not be discouraged and do not lose hope. Put your faith in God, pray without ceasing for your future husband, do what God has asked you to do, and let God do what only He can do.

- *Live in singleness with purpose*

> The thing you should want most is God's kingdom and doing what God wants. Then all these other things you need will be given to you. (Matt. 6:33, ICB)

Although this whole book focuses on finding love, I do not want you to forget that being single is a beautiful and special season that has a very important purpose. It is a time for you to focus on knowing God and developing an intimate love relationship with your Creator. It is also a time for using your abilities and talents that God has given you, for serving Him and serving the needs of others.

The Bible says that the single woman focuses on the things of God, on how to please Him, while the married woman has to think about her earthly responsibilities and how to please her husband; therefore, her interests are divided (1 Cor. 7:32–34). So use the time that God is giving you as a single woman to carry out the purposes and dreams that He has imprinted on your heart and that you can only accomplish with the freedom that singleness provides. Use your time to serve God, to bless other people, and to make a positive change in the lives of others. As you do all these things, your love's promise will come when you least expect it.

This time as a single woman will never come back once you are married. You will not have the same freedom and flexibility that you now enjoy to carry out everything you can achieve right now. So make the most of this season until God gives you the blessing of a husband.

Most importantly, remember that your fulfillment is not in the arms of a man, but in having a love relationship with God and carrying out the purpose He has created you for. Make your relationship with Christ your priority because that is the key to achieving a meaningful life, whether you are single or married. God will fulfill the deepest desires of your heart as you seek Him and completely surrender your life to Him.

Closing

Love is perhaps the most sought after treasure by mankind and the most difficult to find. If I could summarize everything that I have written in this book in one line, it would be the following: *God's love is unconditional, sacrificial, and everlasting; and He is the only reliable way to find this same kind of love in a spouse.*

Love God, seek His direction and follow it, and He will grant the deepest desires of your heart.

If this book has been a blessing to you and if it helps you encounter the love of a special man, I would love to hear your story. I hope that through the pages you have read, God has spoken to your heart, inspired you and strengthened your faith. I am convinced that if you follow His direction, you will be amazed at what He will do for you. Your love story will bring great glory to His Name and will be a testimony and hope for many. Persevere in prayer, keep your body in purity, and allow the Holy Spirit to be your guide always.

I hope that you are able to comprehend how wide, how long, how high, and how deep is the love of Christ for you (Eph. 3:18). It is my prayer that your heart overflows with excitement and expectation as you let God lead your journey to meet the love of your life. If you let God take control, one day you will hold hands with the man that He has chosen to be your husband, and it will be a love like nothing you have experienced before. And when that moment comes, you will be more than ready, equipped, and strong to embrace that next season of your life as a married woman. For now, appreciate the good work that God is doing and wants to accomplish in you as He puts your *Love on Hold*.

For the love you deserve,
Cintia Stirling

INVITATION TO
RECEIVING SALVATION

The *gift* of God is eternal life through Jesus
Christ our Lord. (Rom. 6:23)

Everything you have read in this book is based on my personal relationship with Jesus Christ and the things that He has done in my life. If I hadn't given my life to Him when I was twenty-three years old, I would be completely lost. This book would not have been written, and my love story would not exist. It is because of Him that I have a testimony to share, a purpose, and most importantly, *salvation* and *eternal life*. Maybe you have already given your life to Jesus, but if you haven't, I want you to receive the *gift* of salvation that comes through Him and to experience the unconditional and everlasting love of God.

Let me ask you a question: do you know for sure that you are going to be with God in heaven once this life is over? Just think about it for a moment.

Most people want to go to heaven, but what does it take to secure our place there? The Bible says that eternal life is a *gift* (Rom. 6:23); this means that *you cannot earn it*. No amount of personal effort or good works can get you a place in heaven (Eph. 2:8–9).

Since *we are all sinners*, we do not deserve God's glory, we do not deserve heaven (Rom. 3:23). But God is *merciful*; this means that even though *we are guilty*, He doesn't always issue the punishment we deserve. He *loves us* (Jer. 31:3), and He doesn't want anyone to be lost (2 Pet. 3:9).

However, God is also *just*; and because of His justice, He must *punish* sin (Exod. 34:7). So we have a problem. On one hand, God loves us and doesn't want to punish us; on the other, He is just and must punish sin. Here is the *good news*: God solved this problem by giving His Son, Jesus.

> For God loved the world so much that he gave his only Son. God gave his Son so that *whoever believes in him may not be lost, but have eternal life.* (John 3:16, IBC)

Jesus died on the cross to *pay the penalty* for our sins. Eternal life is a *gift* that is received by *faith in Jesus,* not by works (Eph. 2:8–9). *Saving faith* is to believe and trust that Jesus died for you and that because of Him, you have been saved (Acts 16:31).

However, in order to *receive* the gift of salvation, you need to *accept* it. It is not given to you automatically. You need to *open the door* of your heart and *invite Jesus in* (Rev. 3:20). You need to give Him the "driver's seat" and "control" of your life, not the "back seat." Most importantly, you need to *repent* and turn away from anything that is not pleasant to Him.

Is this what you really want? Do you want to receive salvation? Do you want to be sure that you have eternal life and a place secured in heaven? If your answer is yes, there are two conditions that need to be met: you need to *believe* it in your heart that Jesus is your Savior, and you need to *confess* it with your mouth.

> For it is by *believing in your heart* that you are made right with God, and it is by openly *declaring your faith* that you are saved. (Rom. 10:10, NLT)

If you want to *receive* the gift of eternal life through Jesus Christ, then *call on Him, ask* Him for this *gift* right now.

Here is a suggested prayer:

> Lord Jesus, thank You for Your gift of eternal life. I know I'm a sinner and do not deserve eternal life. But You loved me, so You died and

rose from the grave to purchase a place in heaven
for me. I now trust in You alone for eternal life
and repent from my sins. Please take control as
the Lord of my life and Savior. In Jesus's name.
Amen.

If this prayer is the sincere desire of your heart, you have received
the gift of eternal life. You are now a child of God! Forever!

The story doesn't end here. You need to cultivate your relationship with God from now on daily. It will require effort, time, and
dedication. If you really want to know God intimately, you need to
seek Him. There are several things that you can do to grow in your
relationship and knowledge of God:

- read your Bible,
- pray daily,
- regularly attend a church that honors Jesus and teaches you
  the Bible,
- have fellowship with other Christian believers who will
  help you grow in faith,
- be a witness and tell others what Jesus Christ means to
  you![20]

As you do all of these things, you will be equipped to conquer
and receive all the precious and great promises that God has for your
life. You will also be ready to receive the blessing of a godly husband
and a Christ-centered marriage.

---

[20] *Do You Know*, ©2016 Evangelism Explosion International, Inc., www.evange-
lismexplosion.org, 10 Misty Valley Parkway, Arden, NC 28704-6112.

Discussion Questions

1. Satan seduced Eve with something that *looked good*, was *pleasant,* and *desirable.* How have these characteristics influenced your decision on choosing a partner? What has been the outcome of choosing based on these traits? How differently do you think God would like you to pursue love?

2. What is the impact of pursuing God's love first before pursuing the love of a man? What can you do in order to grow your relationship with God?

3. Singleness is an important season in which God prepares you for His plans and purposes. What has God been doing in your life during this season? How do you think His works will prepare you for the future and for your marriage?

4. From the statistics in chapter 1, we learned that *modern dating* could lead to much pain, heartbreak, and disappointment. Why do you think this is happening? What has been your experience with modern dating? How do you think God's way of finding love can change these realities?

5. In your own words, define what *surrender* means.
    *   Read Genesis 22:1–19 and think about the following: Is there anything or anyone competing for the place in your heart that belongs to God? How will surrendering it prepare you to receive the promises of God?

Apply:

- I encourage you to pursue God's love first before pursuing a love relationship with a man. You can do this by:
    o reading your Bible,
    o praying more,
    o becoming part of a church that helps you grow in your faith.
- Ask God to use this season of singleness as a time to prepare you and equip you His plans and purposes. Ask Him to shape your heart and make it ready to receive the blessing of a husband.
- Surrender to God your desire to be in a love relationship. Allow Him to work on your behalf to introduce you to your future husband.

Discussion Questions

1. Discuss with your group the importance of *praying* for your future husband. How do you think prayer can help you make better decisions about your love life? What kind of *revelation* from the Holy Spirit do you need during this particular time of your life?

2. Discuss what kinds of doubts you have experienced as you wait to meet your future husband. Which ones seem to be the hardest to overcome and why?
   - Read Mark 11:24, Philippians 4:6–7, and James 1:6–8; and identify what these scriptures have in common. How do they change your perception about doubt?

3. Share about a time in which you had to wait before you received an answer to your prayer. How did you feel as you waited? What kind of challenges and fears did you encounter? After your prayer was answered, what can you identify God did during the waiting season?

4. When you pray, there is *spiritual opposition*. This might come in the form of: *intrusive thoughts*, *unresolved issues* from your past, and *sins and temptations*. Which of these apply to your situation? How have they affected your love life?

5. After reading Adriana and Hector's story in chapter 4, what did you learn about the power of praying for your future husband? What did you learn about God's love for people that haven't been saved?

Apply:

This week, you learned about the power of *prayer* and how to pray for your future husband. You also learned about the *spiritual opposition* that might hinder your prayer.

- Ask the Holy Spirit to show you what kind of spiritual opposition might be delaying the answer to your prayers.
- Ask Jesus to deliver you from things from your past that are holding you back. This may include hurts, abuse, sexual sin, and emotional wounds.
- I encourage you to pray for your future husband daily and ask God to prepare both of you for each other.

Discussion Questions

1. *Fear* is contrary to *faith* and is one of the biggest obstacles to finding love. Think about some of your greatest fears as a single woman. Now apply the steps to overcome fear discussed in chapter 5:
    *   Identification—what are you afraid of?
    *   Source—where does this fear come from?
    *   Confrontation—with the help of your group, find scriptures to overcome this fear.
2. Read 2 Timothy 1:7. What can you learn about fear from this scripture? What is the source of all your fears? What do you think is the enemy's goal of inspiring fear in you? What can you do to overcome fear?
3. From what you learned in chapter 6, explain in your own words what is the *spirit of pride*? Has this spirit influenced your decisions and actions? How can this affect your chances of succeeding in love? With the help of scriptures, discuss how you can break the power of pride in your life.
4. This week, you learned there is a *godly independence* and an *ungodly independence*. Explain the difference between them. How do you think your culture has impacted the way people live independently? In what ways can you cultivate *godly independence*?
5. Read 1 John 2:15–17. Discuss with your group the meaning of *lust of the flesh*, *lust of the eyes*, and *the pride of life*. Which of these temptations has had the greatest influence on your love life decisions?

Apply:

Now that you have identified the fears and temptations that you struggle with, pray to the Holy Spirit for:

- *courage* and power to overcome them.
- *humility* to resist the *spirit of pride* and *ungodly independence.*
- *discernment* to recognize evil.

Surrender all your areas of weakness to God and ask Him for strength and wisdom to overcome.

Discussion Questions

1. In your own words, describe what it means to be *unequally yoked*.
    *   Read 2 Corinthians 6:14–15. What does the Bible warn us about being *yoked* together with unbelievers? How does that affect your perspective about dating a believer versus dating an unbeliever?
2. Read Romans 8:5–9. What is the difference between *living according to the flesh* and *living according to the Spirit*? Explain why understanding this is so critical at the moment of choosing a partner. What are some possible outcomes if a person who is *in the realm of the Spirit* joins someone who is *in the realm of the flesh*?
3. Discuss with your group the three ways you can be *unequally yoked*. Have you dated unbelievers or uncommitted believers? If so, what has been your experience?
4. Think about ten qualities you have been looking for when choosing a partner and write them down.
    *   Discuss with your group whether these qualities are found in the Word of God.
    *   What do you need to do to make sure that the qualities you are looking for align with the Word God?
5. Of the *Seven Attributes to Look for in a Husband* described in chapter 9, which ones are the most important to you and why? How has this chapter impacted your perspective about the type of man you would like as a husband?

Apply:

This week, you learned about what it means to be *unequally yoked* and some of the *godly attributes* to look for in a husband.

- Ask the Holy Spirit to lead you in the process of finding a man who is a true believer in Christ.
- Surrender the list of qualities that you have been looking for in a husband and allow God to inspire His thoughts in your heart.
- When you pray for a husband, don't forget to pray for each of the seven attributes you learned in chapter 9.
- Believe that God can bless you with a godly man who truly loves you.

Discussion Questions

1. Share your perspective about premarital sex. Why has society made it acceptable when God's Word clearly is against it? Why do you think God's plan for sex is that people enjoy it exclusively within marriage?

2. Read Ephesians 5:31 and 1 Corinthians 6:17. What is the similarity between these scriptures? How can God's perfect design of *unity* between man and woman be corrupted by premarital sex?

3. This week, you learned how sex creates powerful *emotional bonds*. What is the difference between *godly* and *ungodly emotional bonds*? Have you ever experienced an ungodly emotional bond? If so, how did it affect your mind, your will, and your emotions?

4. According to Galatians 2:20, what is the result of being crucified with Christ? How does our new nature in Christ empower us to overcome sexual immorality and any other kind of sin? According to Matthew 16:24–25, what is required to follow Christ? What does this mean in terms of resisting sexual temptation?

5. Read Philippians 3:13–14. What did Apostle Paul mean by saying, "Forgetting the past and looking forward to what lies ahead"? Have you been dwelling on a past relationship? Share with your group and discuss how this can be affecting your chances of finding love again.

Apply:

- Surrender to God your desire to have sexual intimacy with a man.
- Pray for strength and self-control to resist sexual temptation.
- If you have formed any *ungodly emotional bonds* as a result of sinful relationships or premarital sex, ask the Holy Spirit to break these bonds in the name of Jesus. Pray for deliverance, healing, and restoration for your heart and soul. Ask God to renew your mind and body and to prepare you for your future husband.
- Ask God to help you move on from your past and to look forward to what He has in store for you.

Discussion Questions

1. In chapter 12, you learned about *actions of faith*. Explain in your own words what they are. What is the four-step process for an action of faith? What steps do you think will be the most challenging for you to follow and why?

2. Has God called you to take an action of faith in your love life? If so, what obstacles have you encountered to obey God?

3. Consider the differences between an *action of faith* and an *action in the flesh* described in chapter 12. Which of these actions describe best your approach to finding love? What can you do to cultivate more *actions of faith* and fewer actions *in the flesh*?

4. Of the divine encounters explained in chapter 13, which one did you enjoy reading the most and why? What similarities did you find in these stories? Do you believe that God can prepare a divine encounter between you and your future husband? Why or why not?

5. Discuss with your group at least five traits you found that Rebekah, Rachel, and Ruth had in common. How do you think these characteristics prepared them to receive the blessing of a husband? Which of these traits do you think you need to cultivate more?

Apply:

This week, you learned that an *action of faith* requires a clear instruction from God.

- When you pray, bring your petitions and requests to God and then tune your ear to the Holy Spirit. Give yourself time in silence to hear His voice. Ask Him if there is anything He wants you to do.
- Before every major decision you take in your life, ask God first if He is leading that action.
- Start praying for a divine encounter with the man that God has destined to be your husband.
- Try to cultivate in your life qualities of a godly woman. Learn from the stories of Rebekah, Rachel, and Ruth, and from the virtuous woman described in Proverbs 31.

Discussion Questions

1. In chapter 14, you learned that *paradigms* are concepts we create in our mind about how we want something to be. What kind of paradigms have you created about your future husband? How do you think these paradigms have positively or negatively affected your decisions in love? Do you think that the Holy Spirit has inspired them?

2. Read 1 Samuel 16:7. What does this scripture reveal to you about God's heart? If you were able to focus more on the things God looks at, what impact would that have in your relationships and in your approach for choosing a partner?

3. In what ways has chapter 15 influenced your perception about *honor*? Read Ephesians 6:1–3. Is this scripture challenging for you? If so, why? How can you *honor* God and your parents (or spiritual mentors) with your current and/or future relationships?

4. Discuss with your group your thoughts about the following:
   • Obedience = blessings and reward.
   • Disobedience = problems, torment, and distress.
   Do you agree or disagree? Have you seen this pattern before in your life? If so, please share.

5. Discuss with your group the difference between *worldly dating* and *godly dating* (or courtship.) What dating model have you been following? What has been the result? Which one will you pursue in the future and why?

Apply:

This week, you learned that *paradigms* could be deceitful if not inspired by the Holy Spirit. You also learned about the power of *honor.*

- I encourage you to surrender to God your *paradigms* about what you are looking for in your future husband. Allow the Holy Spirit to inspire His thoughts in you.
- Ask God to help you see beyond people's *physical appearance* and to show you their *heart.* Pray for discernment to recognize your future husband.
- Ask the Holy Spirit who can be a spiritual mentor for you. Be accountable to your parents and spiritual mentors about your love relationships. Seek and follow their direction, advice, wisdom, and correction.
- Pursue *godly dating* rather than *worldly dating.* Pray for wisdom to establish godly dating parameters.

Discussion Questions

1. Discuss with your group the relevance of *purity* in modern dating. Is it seen as something valuable or not? Is *purity* being pursued or has it been forgotten? Why do you think this is the case?

2. What are your thoughts about making a *mutual commitment to purity* with the person are in a relationship with? Will this be challenging for you both? If so, why? How can establishing godly boundaries of physical treatment impact your relationship?

3. Abstaining from sexual intimacy can be challenging if you try to do it alone. Read Ecclesiastes 4:12, and explain the *cord of three strands* and why it is not easily broken? Why is it so powerful to make a commitment to purity in *agreement* with your partner?

4. Everything you have experienced in your life as a single person is part of the journey to your promise. Share how this journey has equipped you and prepared you to receive the blessing of a husband. What areas of your life do you need to work on? What things do you need to surrender to God?

5. In chapter 18, you read about three exhortations to always remember:
   • make God's Word your standard,
   • do not be shaped by this world,
   • live a singleness with purpose.

Discuss with your group what each of these mean to you. How has *Love on Hold* impacted your perspective about how to pursue love and relationships?

Apply:

This week, you learned about the importance of *purity*.

- Ask God to put a desire in your heart to pursue *purity* and *holiness*.
- If you are in a relationship, I encourage you to have *the talk* with your partner to establish physical boundaries that meet God's standards. Pray together. Make a *mutual commitment to purity*.
- If you are single, pray that God will introduce you to a man that respects, appreciates, and supports your desire to pursue purity in your relationship.
- Share with others all you have learned about *Love on Hold* and encourage them to participate on this journey with you.

ABOUT THE AUTHOR

Cintia Stirling is a wife, Christian writer, speaker, and author of *Love on Hold: Waiting on the Man of God.* Her passion is to bring hope, encouragement, and comfort to women in areas of need and struggle. Using biblical truth, storytelling, and testimonies, Cintia equips believers through her books and Bible-study resources.

Born and raised in Mexico, Cintia graduated with a bachelor's degree in international business from ITESM in Monterrey. A one-year study abroad in Canada opened the opportunity for her to work internationally as a market research analyst.

During her years as an analyst, Cintia received the calling from God to write on matters of faith and Christianity, focusing on women's issues. She realized that through her career experience, God was actually equipping her for this ministry.

In 2013, Cintia married her husband, Caleb Stirling, from Austin, Texas; and she moved to the United States. Early in her marriage, she began to pursue God's calling in her life to become a Christian author. In 2019, Cintia released her first book, *Love on Hold: Waiting on the Man of God*; and in 2022 she released the Spanish version, *Amor en Espera: Esperando por el Esposo que Dios tiene para Ti.*

Cintia, her husband, and their two children, Nicole and William, live in San Antonio, Texas. For Cintia it is a privilege to share the

message of *Love on Hold* and *Amor en Espera* in events, conferences, churches and Bible studies.

For more information about the author and how to schedule Cintia to speak at your event, please visit:

www.cintiastirling.com